10 Most
Common Mistakes
Good Parents
Make*

*And How to Avoid Them

Kevin Steede, Ph.D.

PRIMA PUBLISHING

PRIMA PUBLISHING and colophon are registered trademarks of Prima Communications, Inc.

Disclaimer
Although many of the following examples are based on true cases, the names have been changed to respect the privacy of individuals and their families.

Library of Congress Cataloging-in-Publication Data
Steede, Kevin.
  10 most common mistakes good parents make: and how to avoid them / Kevin Steede.
     p.   cm.
  Includes index.
  ISBN 0-7615-1241-1
  1. Child rearing.   2. Parenting.   3. Parent and child.   I. Title.
HQ769.S77   1998
649'.1—dc21   97-43228
                                                                  CIP

  99 00 01 02 HH 10 9 8 7 6 5 4 3 2

Printed in the United States of America

How to Order
Single copies may be ordered from Prima Publishing, P.O. Box 1260BK, Rocklin, CA 95677; telephone (916) 632-4400. Quantity discounts are also available. On your letterhead, include information concerning the intended use of the books and the number of books you wish to purchase.

Visit us online at www.primapublishing.com

To my daughter, Lindsey, who continually reminds me that each new day is a work in progress.

Contents

Introduction

On Being a Parent

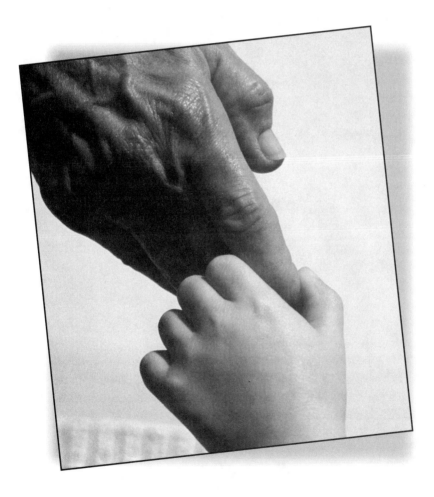

So you are a parent. What does that mean exactly, being a parent? Obviously it means that you were involved in giving birth to a child. Does that define parenthood? Does the act of giving birth make you a parent? I don't think so.

No more important job exists in the world than being a parent. As a psychologist, I have chosen to work with children, teenagers, and their families because I believe so strongly in the crucial role parents play in the lives of their children. I firmly believe that if you choose to bring children into the world, you have a fundamental obligation to actively work to give them the tools to be successful in life. Nothing is more important. Besides, a wise man once said, "You better raise your children right because they are the ones who are going to choose your nursing home!"

Most parents sincerely want to do a good job raising their children. They don't set out to neglect them or cause them harm. In reality, however, many parents get so caught up in their daily routines that parenting takes on a secondary role.

Sadly, they often pay the most attention to their children when problems begin to arise.

Think about it. Most people can tell you what their career goals are. They can rattle off long-term plans for retirement and financial security. They can tell you how many payments are left on the car and how they plan to redecorate the kitchen. Most parents, however, will look at you like you just crawled out from under the refrigerator if you ask them what their plan is for raising happy and healthy children.

Many parents simply haven't thought about it. They assume that if they just go on living their lives as they always have, parenting will take care of itself. They often complain bitterly about how they were raised by their own parents, but they haven't taken the time to really decide how they want to rear their own children. They haven't asked themselves what values they want to communicate to their kids. They haven't discussed the best ways to make sure their children have a strong sense of self. They haven't considered how much time they need to spend with their children or how to make that time available. Many parents just parent in the time that is "left over."

Although I see mothers and fathers who take their parenting role for granted every day, I was always confident that I had avoided this "passive parenting syndrome." As the following story indicates, I am no more immune than anyone else.

As a father, I spend a great deal of time with my daughter, Lindsey. However, I learned a powerful lesson about active parenting one Saturday last year when Lindsey was ten years old.

Being the new owner of an older home (actually, I think the house now owns me), I needed to run a slew of errands.

After rushing through the morning routine, Lindsey and I were off to the office to pick up some checks that needed to go to the bank. Leaving the drive-through, we headed to the nearby cleaners to drop off some clothes. Next came the hardware store and the local nursery.

A hurried lunch at a local fast-food joint led to a flurry of stops, including a grocery store, an electronics store, and a shoe store. A quick stop at home yielded to the car wash, the service station, and a bookstore.

Home again, I prepared dinner while Lindsey watched television. After dinner, she hustled off to the shower while I repaired an uppity appliance. After washing up, I headed to Lindsey's room to find her reading a book.

Sitting down beside her, I asked her if she was ready for bed. She looked up from her book and said, "You know, Daddy, I wish we could spend more time together. I really miss doing that."

Her statement really rocked me—and she was absolutely right. Although we had physically spent the entire day together, mentally we had been miles apart. Like many of my clients who struggle with being a good parent, I had fallen into the trap of letting life get in the way of raising my child.

Children need to know that their parents are *actively* experiencing life with them, not just passively taking them along for the ride. When parents are consciously aware of this simple fact, they have taken a huge step toward teaching their children to be happy, self-motivated, and independent adults. Conversely, taking time with

Children need to know that their parents are *actively* experiencing life with them, not just passively taking them along for the ride.

our children for granted can prompt them to be driven, pre-occupied, and self-absorbed.

The following Saturday I was again confronted with a daunting list of "to-do's." Determined not to repeat the mistakes of the previous weekend, I consciously altered the game plan. Instead of rushing through breakfast, we made it special by eating on the patio. We still had to run the errands, but Lindsey brought along a tape so that we could sing in the car. We also had a contest to see who could spot the most VW Beetles, cars she refers to as "slug-bugs."

Back at home, I had to make several more repairs, this time on the wiring. However, instead of sending Lindsey off to play, I involved her in the project. She had great fun learning to use the power screwdriver and was very proud that she was able to help her dad.

After the repairs were completed, we took time to take a bike ride around the neighborhood. It was amazing to watch her joy in such a simple pleasure. After the ride, she helped me prepare dinner and clean up afterward. Dinner took a bit longer, as a result, but Lindsey felt involved and valued.

After her shower, we sat in the backyard on a blanket trying to pick out the various stars and constellations. Much of the time was spent looking at the sky without a word passing between us.

Then it became time to go to bed. I was tucking her in when she said, "Daddy, this was one of the best days ever. I love you." I don't think she saw my tears.

Lindsey in all her ten-year-old wisdom had reminded me (and I thought I was supposed to be teaching *her*) that just by being more aware and more proactive as a parent, I made a major difference in her life. Just by changing my focus, I was able to turn a potentially rushed and harried day into one to be treasured. Perhaps a few things were left undone, but the reward was well worth it.

Try a little experiment. Sit down with your children and ask them a question. Ask them what are the most important things that they have learned from you. You may be surprised at the result. Lindsey answered, "To be nice to others, to believe in myself, to not take things too seriously, and that cheese is the best!" Oh well, three out of four isn't too bad.

Being a parent is not something that you *are*—it is something that you *do.* Parenting involves action. It involves making decisions about what you want your children to know about life, about relationships, about honesty, about honor. It involves taking specific steps to help children place a high value on their own personal character. Being a parent is about taking active steps to teach your children how to become independent and responsible adults.

> **B**eing a parent is not something that you *are*—it is something that you *do.*

I do see a significant number of mothers and fathers who have made the decision to be active parents. These are individuals who put a premium on being at the school play or spending time with their children instead of playing golf or working on Saturday morning. These are parents who recognize that being a mother or father is the most important job in their lives.

I don't mean to imply that being a good parent means spending all of your time dealing with your children. Many parents live very hectic and pressured lives. It's necessary for some parents to work multiple jobs, and others don't have the benefit of a caring spouse who can lend a hand.

What I am suggesting is that we need to learn to think about parenting differently. We need to strike a balance among our jobs, our need for relaxation, and our roles as parents. We must choose to make parenting an active priority, not simply something we do when we have some extra time.

It is for these people who have chosen to be active parents that this book is written. It is a simple book designed to help guide parents through common parenting pitfalls. It is designed to help them develop a positive attitude and dynamic and effective parenting skills.

Each chapter outlines common parenting problems that I encounter daily in my practice. The effective, commonsense strategies are the same ones that people pay hundreds of dollars to learn in a psychologist's office. Included at the end of each chapter is a checklist of the major points outlined in that chapter. A self-test is also included at the end of each chapter to help refresh your memory and assure that you understood and retained important points.

Anyone can be a great parent. It takes only the desire to make parenting a priority in your life. It also helps to know some of the strategies and skills outlined in this book. Read on. . . .

Planting
Mental Mines

Most of us want the absolute best for our children. We discipline, encourage, and counsel them so that they can successfully navigate the often treacherous waters of childhood and adolescence. We would never knowingly do anything that would harm or hurt them.

In our zeal to provide effective life skills and a solid value system, we can sometimes instill other, less positive beliefs in our children, often without being aware of it. These "mental mines" can have profound effects in later life.

As parents, we have our own set of biases, often gleaned from our own childhood experiences. While many of these assumptions about life are positive and beneficial, many of them negatively impact our lives. The best way to avoid passing on negative and nonproductive mental mines to our children is to recognize them in ourselves and in our own parenting style. This chapter will discuss some of the more common mental mines.

Mental Mine 1: "I must be good at everything."

Most parents certainly want to encourage their children to do their best at the tasks that they attempt in life. They want them to feel free to explore their unique talents and interests. However, in spite of their good intentions, some parents may actually be sending unintended messages to their children.

A very fine line exists between motivating children to *do* their best and promoting the mistaken belief that children must *be* the best at everything that they attempt. This mental mine is planted when we push children into activities in which they have little or no interest. It also gets planted in the minds of our kids when less-than-ideal performance at a given activity is always considered unacceptable.

As this mental mine is incorporated into a child's belief system, his or her self-esteem begins to erode. There is simply no way that a child can be "the best" at everything. Children who feel that they must be the best quickly come to believe that they have somehow let down their parents and, ultimately, themselves. Adults in whom this mental mine was implanted as children may become angry at the demands placed on them or depressed because they feel as though they can never measure up to what others expect of them.

To avoid the effects of this mental mine, children need to be exposed to a variety of activities and encouraged to explore further those that interest them.

> A very fine line exists between motivating children to *do* their best and promoting the mistaken belief that children must *be* the best at everything that they attempt.

They need to understand that each person has different interests and abilities, that each person has a unique combination of strengths and weaknesses.

A mother brought her son and his sister into my office because she thought that something was wrong with them. Her eight-year-old son, who was rather small, was showing no interest in sports. He apparently preferred to spend time on the computer and was quite talented in that area. This distraught mother's daughter, on the other hand, loved athletic activity and shied away from more traditional female roles.

The parents of these children had spent a great deal of time and energy trying to force the son into sports and discouraging the daughter from the activities she enjoyed. The result was two unhappy children who felt badly about themselves when they were unable to succeed in their parents' chosen activities. My advice was to let these children find their own way and spend time doing activities in which they showed interest and talent.

This mother called my office several years later and informed me that her daughter had just won the city track meet and that her son had recently written a computer game program that was being reviewed by a large corporation for possible distribution! The moral to this story is that children should be encouraged to explore their own interests and strengths, not those that we, as parents, wish for them.

Although the benefits of encouraging a child's unique talents may seem quite obvious, many parents push their children in one direction or another for a variety of reasons. It may be that a parent excelled at a particular activity and wishes to see a carbon copy of himself or herself in a child. Perhaps the parent was "less than perfect" in a given area and pushes a child to compensate for his or her own short-comings. Some well-intentioned parents live vicariously through their children to enrich their own lives.

The Dawsons represent a rather extreme example. They came to me seeking help with their ten-year-old son, Ben. Mr. and Mrs. Dawson were both high achievers and quite successful financially. Their concern over their son's recent drop in grades was quite genuine.

They were quick to tell me that Ben was not a behavioral problem at school. His marks in conduct were always very good. Ben also was generally well behaved at home, except when it came to anything school related. He frequently "forgot" to bring home his assignments and was very resistant to the idea of doing his homework. Getting him to sit down each night to begin his assignments was becoming increasingly difficult.

At this point in the conversation, I began considering a host of possible causes for Ben's academic slump. Was it possible he had an attention-deficit disorder? Had anything occurred in the family that would cause him recent emotional distress? Perhaps he was depressed.

To begin to sort through the various possibilities, I began to ask some specific questions, starting with Ben's history at school. Had Ben always been a good student? They informed me he had. When did they notice Ben's grades begin to drop? Actually, they noticed it with the last report card. What grades had fallen and by how much? Imagine my surprise when they told me, with somber expressions, that his grade in math had taken a precipitous drop, from 98 to 92!

It didn't take a genius to deduce that Ben's parents were putting a tremendous amount of pressure on him to succeed. Ben clearly felt that no matter what he did, it would not be good enough for his parents—and he was probably right.

They not only wanted him to do well, but they wanted perfection from their ten-year-old son.

Since he felt he was going to disappoint them anyway, Ben began to rebel. His understandable insecurity about not pleasing his parents led to passive-aggressive attempts to deflect responsibility for his less-than-perfect grades. He would rather not do his homework than risk an imperfect performance. He would rather forget an assignment than risk his parent's disapproval for anything less than a perfect grade.

It took some doing, but the Dawsons began to understand the pressure they were exerting on their son. I recommended that they have a little talk with Ben and assure him that they loved him whatever grades he brought home. I further suggested that they tell him that they trust him to be in charge of his own academics and that they wouldn't push him anymore. They assured him that they would be available if he needed help but that it would be his responsibility to ask.

The strategy worked. Within three weeks, Ben was coming home from school and doing his homework without complaint. He became less sullen at home, and his grades stayed high. He felt much happier, and his self-esteem skyrocketed because he was making his grades because *he* wanted to, not because he was being pushed.

Parents, like the Dawsons, can avoid planting the "I have to be the best" mental mine and promote and child's sense of self by praising a child for trying, not for whether the child was successful. Reinforcing children's

Reinforcing children's *effort* at a task rather than their *level of achievement* will increase self-esteem and motivation to attempt future activities.

effort at a task rather than their *level of achievement* will increase self-esteem and motivation to attempt future activities. Encourage children to give their best effort, and judge the success based on how hard they tried.

Mental Mine 2: "I am my achievements."

This mental mine is a close cousin of mental mine 1. Once again, this belief is incorporated as a result of parents' desire for their children to do well at the things that they attempt. We all want our children to succeed and to feel good about themselves.

It is important to understand, however, that children have a difficult time differentiating between approval or disapproval of *what they do* versus *who they are* as individuals. In other words, a parent's approval of a particular accomplishment may be interpreted by a child to mean that a parent loves them. The reverse is also true. Parental disapproval of an action can be experienced by a child as rejection or withdrawal of love. This tendency is particularly true of younger children.

Children desperately need to know that a parent loves and approves of them, independent of the successes or failures of the moment. This critical concept is called "unconditional love." In a nutshell, unconditional love means that our children know that absolutely nothing would ever result in us withdrawing our love. We may approve or disapprove of *specific behaviors*, but our love of that child is unwavering.

My clients often respond to this concept with statements like "Of course my child knows that we love her." My response is always "*How* does she know?" Again, a child has difficulty telling the difference between a parent being angry and a parent not loving or liking them anymore. It is a parent's responsibility to make sure the child understands the difference and knows that he or she is loved unconditionally.

Parents can communicate unconditional love to a child in a variety of ways. Whenever possible, make sure that your approval or disapproval of specific behaviors is distinct from your love of your child. Especially with younger children, you may have to actually verbalize this distinction. If a child breaks a prized vase, for example, it may be helpful to say, "I'm not angry at you, Sean. I'm just frustrated because I've had that vase a long time."

It is also helpful to show approval or disapproval of *behaviors,* not people. Statements such as "You are such a good boy" or "You have been horrible today" are not effective in changing behavior and do promote confusion between love and approval. Saying "I liked the way you helped with the dishes without being asked" or "I'm angry that you didn't take out the trash" is more effective and much clearer than making more global statements. Being sure to tell your child that you love them when they have not done anything particularly noteworthy will also send the message that your love is not based on your child's performance.

I saw the damage that not understanding the concept of unconditional love can do when I was watching my daughter play basketball. One little girl on the other team made a bad pass to one of her teammates, causing the ball to go out of bounds. The coach on the other team immediately called a time-out and began to yell at her. The child was visibly shaken.

Throughout the game, the coach got increasingly angry at this girl, yelling at her across the court. Eventually, he began to call her names like "stupid" and "lazy." By the end of the game, he would not even look at this girl who was by now crying uncontrollably. It turned out that this coach was the girl's father!

What do you think this child learned about performance and achievement? How do you think this episode affected her self-esteem?

Again, when love appears conditional, it has particularly negative effects on younger children. About a year ago I attended a birthday party at a neighbor's home. Everyone was sitting in the den laughing and joking. The couple in whose home the party was being held had just put their three-year-old son to bed.

Half an hour later, the toddler wandered back into the room. Clearly irritated, his father barked, "Damn it, I told you to stay in bed!" The toddler quickly retreated.

After several minutes, I excused myself to go to the restroom. As I rounded the corner, I found the little boy sitting in the hall crying. When I stopped to ask him why he was crying, he shyly turned his tear-streaked face toward mine and asked, "Do you think my daddy loves me?"

Although these examples are rather dramatic, they clearly demonstrate the effects of not communicating unconditional love to your children. Even more subtle instances of making parental love appear conditional can have a cumulative negative impact on our children.

Children who consistently feel a parent's unconditional love become more secure and have a much higher self-esteem. They become more confident of their worth and begin to rely more on their own internal resources. Conversely, children who feel that a parent's love is conditional feel insecure and depend more on external approval for validation.

This reliance on external sources for their sense of worth makes them far more vulnerable to peer-pressure. Many adults who have experienced love that is *conditional* obsessively seek approval through career advancement or changing relationships. They never seem to be able to get enough approval. They never seem to *be* good enough. Unfortunately, these individuals have been taught to define themselves by their achievements.

Children who consistently feel a parent's unconditional love become more secure and have a much higher self-esteem. They become more confident of their worth and begin to rely more on their own internal resources.

On the other hand, children who have been showered with unconditional love appear quite different. Their lightheartedness, confidence, and ability to tolerate frustration easily distinguish these children. They are more outgoing and more willing to attempt new things.

Adults who have received unconditional love as children tend to be more secure and "centered." They are better at taking criticism and much better at relying on themselves, rather than others, for their sense of self-worth. Showing children unconditional love is, simply put, a wonderful investment in our kids. It's free, it's fun, and it works!

Mental Mine 3:
"Negative emotions are bad."

Two of the most common problems that I see in my practice involve wives who complain that their husbands are emotionally distant and husbands who complain that their wives have difficulty appropriately expressing anger and resentment. Invariably, when we explore these issues in more depth, we clearly discover that these individuals have incorporated powerful messages that it is inappropriate to express strong "negative" emotions such as anger, disappointment, frustration, or grief. The result is an adult who is emotionally constricted or plagued by guilt.

Take the case of Don and Brenda. This couple, both in their late twenties, came to my office to discuss their vastly different parenting styles. Brenda tended to encourage their two young sons to express their emotions freely. After losing a Little League baseball game, for example, Brenda actively encouraged her sons to share their disappointment and frustration. If they were unable to articulate their feelings, she was willing to simply hold them while they cried.

Brenda's approach clearly infuriated Don. He often made statements such as, "Brenda, stop coddling those boys. They need to learn how to handle it when things don't go their way." He seemed to get enraged and disgusted when his sons displayed such "weak" emotions.

The owner of a small carpet company, Don appeared to be aloof and indifferent to his employees. When his secretary lost her young son in an auto accident, Don made himself scarce, clearly uncomfortable with her frequent emotional outpourings. Even Brenda relied primarily on her friends and family when she needed to express any amount of significant emotion.

Don was also brought up in a household where emotional expression was not encouraged. The son of a factory supervisor and one of eight children, he found that his father was largely unavailable to him. When his father, a strict disciplinarian, was at home, he was often tired and irritable. He tended to view life as hard and uncompromising; consequently, he demanded his children be "tough" in order to meet the challenge.

Parents often plant the "negative emotions are bad" mental mine in their children because they themselves are uncomfortable with emotional expression and therefore unable to provide adequate role models for their own children. Their own inability to express and respond adequately to strong emotions is then, unfortunately, communicated to their children. They may also actively inhibit expression of anger or fear by invalidating a child's emotional state.

Clearly, statements like "Boys don't cry" or "You shouldn't be angry with her" inhibit normal emotional expression. Of course boys cry, and it is normal and healthy to be angry. Just as damaging are more subtle statements such as "Don't worry about it, you'll do fine." Each of these parental comments could communicate to children that they do not have the right to feel a given emotion or that what they're feeling is not very important.

In an effort to make their children feel better, parents sometimes unwittingly dismiss or invalidate the feelings of their children. Judy fell into this trap with her fourteen-year-old daughter Tiffany.

Tiffany came home from school one afternoon visibly upset.

JUDY: What's the matter, honey? You look upset.

TIFFANY: [Beginning to cry] Oh, Mom, Brad told me he doesn't want to go steady anymore. He likes that dumb old Alice. He even asked her to go to the dance next month!

JUDY: [Putting her arm around her daughter, a faint smile on her face] Oh, honey, don't worry about it. I never liked that Brad very much anyway. And

> besides, you'll find another nice boy to take to the
> dance in no time.

Unfortunately, in her haste to comfort her child, Judy probably gave her the message that she shouldn't be feeling sad about her boyfriend leaving her. In fact, being sad when a boyfriend leaves is a perfectly natural response. Judy should have first acknowledged and validated her daughter's feelings before attempting to comfort her.

In truth, everyone experiences a wide variety of emotions, some more pleasant than others. Further, it is normal and natural to feel strong "negative" emotions such as anger or fear. I learned this lesson in graduate school.

When I went to graduate school, I was suddenly associated with a variety of individuals who had a major trait in common: they were exceptionally smart. They all seemed to know exactly what they were doing and were very poised as they went about their daily activities. This cool and calm demeanor was especially true for Melinda. She seemed to handle each challenge without missing a beat. I, on the other hand, felt as though at any moment Melinda and the other students would see how afraid I was and realize that I must be a fraud, that I didn't really belong there.

As chance would have it, I was placed in a graduate student office with Melinda and two other students. After our second week of being in the same office, Melinda suddenly turned to me and said, "Kevin, how do you do it? You seem to always know what you're doing and nothing seems to get to you." Imagine my surprise! It was at that moment that I knew that *everyone* experiences fear and insecurity.

Our goal as parents should be to communicate to our children that they have a right to feel anything they wish and that strong feelings are perfectly normal. They happen to everyone. There may be appropriate and inappropriate ways to *express* those feelings, but experiencing them is perfectly normal and healthy. The more comfortable our children are with their emotions, the more open and giving they can be in future relationships.

Our goal as parents should be to communicate to our children that they have a right to feel anything they wish and that strong feelings are perfectly normal.

Mental Mine 4: "Everyone must like me."

Julie, an attractive woman in her mid-twenties, tearfully recounted her recent experience with a blind date. The young man arrived to pick her up and announced that he had abruptly changed the plans for the date. At dinner he ordered the meal without consulting her and smoked at the table without asking if she minded. He spent much of the date talking on his cellular telephone and the remaining time talking about himself. Not surprisingly, Julie had a terrible time. Yet, here she was in my office crying because he hadn't called her back for another date. She was wondering what she had done wrong!

Jason, another client, called me one afternoon in a panic. He breathlessly described an incident that had occurred that day at work. Jason was working with a colleague on a joint project. On the morning before the completed project was to be presented to their supervisor, Jason had noticed a part of the summary assigned to his colleague was missing. When he pointed out the omission to his associate, he became angry and snapped at Jason. Jason, although clearly in the right, was full of anxiety and remorse because his associate's anger at him *obviously* meant that he had done something wrong.

These scenarios have something in common. Both Julie and Jason were desperately looking for someone else's approval to make themselves feel adequate. In seeking this external validation, they were willing to doubt their own motivations, impressions, and actions. Julie and Jason both rely on others to make them feel good about themselves.

As children, we are naturally taught to try to get along with other people. We are given strong messages to conform to the wishes of our parents, our teachers, and others in positions of authority. We are also encouraged to play in harmony with our peers and to avoid conflict whenever possible.

Girls in our society are especially vulnerable to this message. As much as we may try to minimize sex-role stereotypes, differences in the messages we give our male and female children remain. Parents still tend to encourage competitiveness and achievement to a greater degree in boys. Girls tend to be conditioned to be more congenial and nurturing, even by parents who try to avoid such distinctions.

So what's the problem, Doc? Is there anything wrong with teaching our children to be nice? Shouldn't we teach our kids to get along?

Of course we should. It is important to teach our children to get along and conform to authority when necessary. The problem arises when the teaching goes no further. It is important to balance this need to accommodate others with an understanding that some conflict is inevitable and normal. Further, our children need to be taught how to express their own feelings appropriately and to feel confident in that expression.

Children who grow up with the mindset that they must please everyone will be full of self-doubt and anxiety. Their feeling of self-worth will be solely under the control of others. If you like me, I'm OK. If you don't like me, something must be wrong with me. Both children and adults who base their self-worth on the opinions of others alone are vulnerable to abusive relationships, peer pressure, and other exploitive situations.

Letting children know that they can't and shouldn't please everyone will help avoid this mental mine. Parents should communicate to children that some conflict is inevitable and that, although they should listen to alternative viewpoints, they should "stick to their guns" if they feel that they are in the right.

Agreeing to let children disagree with us, as parents, from time to time can communicate that a child's feelings and desires are important and worthwhile, even if they don't conform to our own. A recent situation involving a friend of mine provides a good illustration.

Craig was approached by his eleven-year-old son, Arnie, for permission to buy a trampoline, which was apparently quite the rage in their neighborhood. Several of his friends had recently acquired one.

Craig was understandably reluctant. Although Arnie had the necessary money saved, Craig was

> **P**arents should communicate to children that some conflict is inevitable and that, although they should listen to alternative viewpoints, they should "stick to their guns" if they feel that they are in the right.

concerned that he would quickly tire of the trampoline and regret spending the money. He explained his reservations to his son, but Arnie remained resolute.

Craig then tried a time-tested parenting skill—delay. But after several weeks, Arnie was still determined. He was even performing odd jobs around the house to earn extra money.

Finally, Craig relented. He informed his son that, because he had remained so consistently adamant, he would take him to the sporting goods store. Arnie looked at his father and asked, "So, Dad, do you think it's a good idea to buy it now?" Craig wisely replied, "No, Son, I still feel the same, but you seem to feel strongly about it, so I'm going to let you make your own decision."

By letting his son express his own opinion on this small matter, even though it is different from his own, Craig communicated to his son that his opinion had value. His decision probably went a long way toward making his son a more confident and self-sufficient adult.

By empowering our children to have faith in their own beliefs and opinions, even in the face of disapproval by others, we strengthen their ability to resist peer-pressure. A teenager who has learned his lesson is far more likely to say no when his friends ask him to smoke a joint after school. An adolescent who has learned to stand firm in the face of opposition is less likely to be pressured into having sex before she is ready.

Mental Mine 5: "It is wrong to make mistakes or ask for help."

One of my own personal childhood lessons about making mistakes occurred at the dinner table when one of us would spill a glass of milk. Being a rather stern man, my stepfather would immediately leap up from his chair and yell at the offender, fixing him with a withering look. The accident was quickly elevated to the status of a capital crime, and the unfortunate child was left feeling shamed and on the verge of tears.

Obviously, a strong message about making mistakes was communicated to the children in my family. In essence, mistakes were to be avoided at all costs or covered up when they did occur.

Perhaps as a result of this lesson, I try very hard to help my daughter learn from her mistakes. If attaching unnecessary shame and guilt to a mistake can be avoided, the experience can provide a profitable lesson. From an early age, my daughter learned where we kept the paper towels and how to refill her glass of milk!

Simply put, making mistakes is a part of the human condition, a fact that is unlikely to change anytime soon. Children who understand that mistakes are natural and unavoidable will feel a greater level of self-acceptance. They will avoid the self-defeating tendency to blame themselves for the inherently trial-and-error process that is life.

Joan realized the importance of this lesson while putting her nine-year-old daughter, Meagan, to bed one evening. As Meagan was climbing into bed, she unexpectedly looked at her mother and burst into tears. When Joan, surprised, asked her what was wrong, Meagan sputtered, "I'm so stupid, Mommy. I failed a math test today." The anguish on her face was unmistakable.

After Joan put her arms around her daughter to calm her, the story began to unfold. Meagan, generally an A student, had gotten confused and studied the wrong material for her test. Consequently, she had failed the test.

Rather than criticize Meagan for her mistake, Joan wisely assured her that everyone makes mistakes. She then asked her whether there was anything that Meagan might do to prevent this error in the future. After agreeing to talk a little less and pay more attention to the assignments, Meagan, much relieved, snuggled under the covers.

As she was leaving the room, Joan turned and asked, "Meagan, how do you think you would have done if you were tested on the material you did study?" Meagan's tiny voice, muffled by her pillow, replied, "I would've aced it, of course."

By emphasizing the fact that mistakes are to be expected and learned from, Joan better prepared her daughter to face future disappointments and setbacks. By helping her accept and profit from her natural fallibility, this wise mother also helped her daughter feel better about herself, thereby increasing her self-esteem.

Closely related to this concept is the notion that asking for help is a sign of incompetence and weakness. In our desire to help our children be self-sufficient, independent adults, we may inadvertently plant a mental mine that says "I have to do it all myself." In a world as wonderfully complicated as ours, it is a rare individual who can live independently of others' help.

My younger brother owns and manages several restaurants and nightclubs. One day we were discussing a restaurant that was opening soon. I was amazed at the number of details, both large and small, involved in such an opening. The number of permits, licenses, vendors, and so forth, that had to be obtained was staggering. He also had to deal with employees, paperwork, stock, and the building itself. As I listened to this litany in utter amazement, I had to stop him and ask, "How on earth do you know how to do all these things?

It seems overwhelming." He looked at me with a slightly puzzled expression and said, "I don't, of course, but I find people who do." My brother had definitely learned that knowing your limitations and when to ask for assistance is an adaptive and necessary skill.

Parents can develop this skill in their children by providing a safe and supportive atmosphere at home. When a child asks a question, the parents should make it clear that the inquiry is welcome and will be considered. Statements such as "You know, that's a good question. Let's think about that" can reinforce a sense of safety and promote inquisitiveness and curiosity. If a supportive atmosphere is nurtured in the home, children are likely to carry this sense of empowerment and safety into the world.

> If a supportive atmosphere is nurtured in the home, children are likely to carry this sense of empowerment and safety into the world.

Things to Remember
Planting Mental Mines

- Mental mines are unhealthy messages that parents convey to their children that can become negative and destructive as children mature.
- Some mental mines to be avoided are:
    I must be good at everything.
    I am my achievements.
    Having strong emotions is bad.
    Everyone must like me.
    It is wrong to make mistakes or ask for help.

When parents teach their children to assess a situation and ask for assistance when necessary, they increase their children's chances of success. A child who is not afraid to ask a question in class will make better grades, for example. By learning this valuable skill, children can learn to draw on a vast array of resources to accomplish their goals. They will ultimately feel less isolated and alone, quickly building confidence and a sense of competence.

Self-Test 1

Please read each of the following five examples to determine which mental mine is associated with it.

1. "Honey, that's wonderful. You got all A's on your report card. I really love you!"
   A. I must be good at everything.
   B. I am my achievements.
   C. Negative emotions are bad.
   D. Everyone must like me.
   E. It's wrong to make mistakes or ask for help.

2. "Now, listen, Son, I know that practicing the piano is hard work, but I learned to like it and so can you."
   A. I must be good at everything.
   B. I am my achievements.
   C. Negative emotions are bad.
   D. Everyone must like me.
   E. It's wrong to make mistakes or ask for help.

3. "But, Mom, Sally said that she doesn't want to play with me anymore. I think she's upset because I played with Nancy yesterday."

   "Listen, Honey, you need to go and tell Sally that you are sorry. You don't want her to be mad at you, do you?"

A. I must be good at everything.
B. I am my achievements.
C. Negative emotions are bad.
D. Everyone must like me.
E. It's wrong to make mistakes or ask for help.

4. "Granddad, would you help me put this model together?"
    "No, Son, I can't help you with the model. I made your father put his models together all by himself. That's how I taught him to be a man."
    A. I must be good at everything.
    B. I am my achievements.
    C. Negative emotions are bad.
    D. Everyone must like me.
    E. It's wrong to make mistakes or ask for help.

5. "Now, Mike, don't get so upset. I'm sure you'll do fine on the test tomorrow."
    A. I must be good at everything.
    B. I am my achievements.
    C. Negative emotions are bad.
    D. Everyone must like me.
    E. It's wrong to make mistakes or ask for help.

6. What is the best way to avoid planting mental mines in children?
    A. Watch more *Jerry Springer.*
    B. Attempt to correct them only when absolutely necessary.
    C. Recognize mental mines in ourselves and our own parenting styles.

7. The critical concept that involves children understanding that their parents love them *no matter what* is called:
    A. Paradigm shift.
    B. Unconditional love.
    C. Unrequited love.

Self-Test Answers

1. "Honey, that's wonderful. You got all A's on your report card. I really love you."

   Answer B: This parent's statement implies that her love for her child is based on how well she does in school.

2. "Now, listen, Son, I know that practicing the piano is hard work, but I learned to like it and so can you."

   Answer A: This statement implies that if the child does not like and excel at playing the piano, something is wrong with him.

3. "But, Mom, Sally said that she doesn't want to play with me anymore. I think she's upset because I played with Nancy yesterday."

   "Listen, Honey, you need to go and tell Sally that you are sorry. You don't want her to be mad at you, do you?"

   Answer D: This response implies that because Sally is mad, the child must have done something wrong.

4. "Granddad, would you help me put this model together?"

   "No, Son, I can't help you with the model. I made your father put his models together all by himself. That's how I taught him to be a man."

   Answer E: The grandfather communicated to the boy that he would be "less than a man" if he were helped with his project.

5. "Now, Mike, don't get so upset. I'm sure you'll do fine on the test tomorrow."

   Answer C: Mike got the message that it is not normal to be anxious before a big test.

6. What is the best way to avoid planting mental mines in children?

Answer C: If parents recognize their own irrational beliefs, they will be more sensitive to the need to avoid planting these mental mines in their children.

7. The critical concept that involves children understanding that their parents love them *no matter what* is called:

Answer B: Unconditional love, which communicates to children that they have value and worth, independent of how they behave at any given time.

Requiring Children to Misbehave

A*ll kids want attention.* This simple statement is a fundamental parenting truth. Children thrive on positive attention from their parents, but they will make do with negative attention. They would love for you as a parent to praise them, but they would rather have you yelling at them or correcting them than ignoring them altogether. Children despise being ignored.

Unfortunately, parents tend to get caught up in the hustle and bustle of their daily lives and forget to praise their children when they are doing well and staying out of trouble. Instead, they wait until the kids do something wrong, and then they give them plenty of attention. In effect, the process requires children to misbehave to win parental attention.

Many parents come to my office complaining that their children are engaging in any number of misbehaviors. Upon closer examination, these problems are often maintained by parents focusing solely on their children's bad behavior. In essence, they are unwittingly reinforcing such behavior with their attention.

Terry seemed to be constantly fighting with her two-year-old brother. Her parents are always admonishing her to leave him alone or to "play nice." They talked to her, they chastised her, and yet the behavior persisted. Out of sheer frustration, they usually ended up yelling at her and sending her to her room.

Feeling displaced by her younger sibling, Terry was too young to know how to ask for the attention she desperately needed from her parents. However, she did know how to misbehave with her brother, which, in turn, solicited the desired parental attention.

To be more effective, parents need to learn to look for positive behaviors exhibited by their children and then reward those behaviors with attention and praise. It sounds like a simple process, but it takes considerable effort to remember to look for and reward positive behaviors. It is very easy to fall back into the trap of "not rocking the boat" and remaining silent when children are behaving well.

> Parents need to learn to look for positive behaviors exhibited by their children and then reward those behaviors with attention and praise. It sounds like a simple process, but it takes considerable effort to remember to look for and reward positive behaviors.

In Terry's case, the problem with her brother was fairly easily fixed. Her parents were taught to pay attention to the times when Terry was *not* tormenting her brother. On those occasions, her parents were to compliment how well she played with him and how proud they were of her. Her parents had to change their focus from concentrating on the problem behavior to directing their attention toward those times that she behaved well. Within a week, Terry's behavior markedly improved.

As part of my internship, I was employed on the adolescent unit of a state hospital. The teenage patients would arrive on the unit and be placed on level 1. If they followed the unit rules, they could rise through levels 2 and 3, ultimately being placed on level 4, from which they could be discharged. The higher levels carried more privileges such as weekend passes, free time, and points to be used at the patient store. When I initially arrived on the unit, the majority of the patients were clustered on the lowest two levels. Very few teenagers were on level 3 or 4. Within a few days it quickly became clear why this was the case.

Each morning the staff held a meeting to discuss each patient's progress the day before. The teens were called one at a time into the meeting room. The staff would spend a great deal of time with the patients that had behaved inappropriately because there were many notes on the chart to discuss. Those students who had behaved appropriately and followed the unit rules were given a quick "keep up the good work" and were quickly sent out to get the next patient.

I suggested that we begin to reward appropriate behavior by spending at least as much time with patients who had cooperated with their program as we did with those that had caused problems. Within two weeks, 60 percent of the unit had moved up to levels 3 and 4, a dramatic improvement. And the only change that was made was a slight shift in focus, away from negative behaviors and onto more positive ones.

Rewarding positive behaviors really works. To be most effective, the parental praise needs to be directed toward *specific behaviors* rather than expressed in more global positive statements. It is much more effective to say "Thank you for answering the door" than to say "You've really been a good kid today."

One of my clients has a twelve-year-old son, Calvin. Calvin had an annoying habit of dropping his book bag, shoes, and coat on the living room floor each day after school. His mother would remind him, scold him, and ground him, all to no avail. Calvin's things still ended up on the living room floor. She was, in fact, rewarding him with her attention each time he dropped his things on the floor.

At my suggestion, this frustrated mother began to look for the times when Calvin actually carried his things to his room. As with most cases of this sort, the incidences of positive behavior were few and far between, but they did occur. In the meantime, she would simply gather the dropped items and put them in the garage where it was inconvenient for Calvin to retrieve them each morning before school.

After several days, she "caught" Calvin going through the living room without dropping anything. She went up to him, gave him a little hug, and thanked him for being so considerate. Calvin's initial surprise quickly gave way to a look of pride and accomplishment. Because he got positive attention for putting his things in his room, he continued to make an effort to do so. His mother still remembers to thank him from time to time.

Another young client was constantly forgetting to bring supplies home from school. He either forgot his assignment, book, or entire backpack. His parents were understandably concerned. They came to my office hoping that I would give their son a battery of psychological tests to determine what was wrong.

Instead, I suggested that they try a little experiment. On those rare occasions when he did remember to bring everything home, they were to tell him how proud they were and how responsible they thought he was being. If he brought everything home two times in a row, they were to reward him with something tangible such as a trip to the ice cream store. This young man improved dramatically within a week, and I never did give him that battery of tests.

Sometimes a child simply does not possess the skills or the knowledge required to perform a given task. If a child doesn't know how to do a task, how can he or she be rewarded? Occasionally, it may be necessary to reward small steps toward a particular goal.

For example, I wanted my daughter, Lindsey, to begin to make her bed when she was about four years old. First, I showed her how to make the bed and suggested that she give it a try the next morning. When I arrived to check on her attempt, I discovered that she had gotten the covers about halfway on the bed. I praised her effort by saying, "That's a good first try, honey. I'm proud of you. Tomorrow how about trying to get the covers all the way on the bed, like this." I again demonstrated the proper technique. The next morning, Lindsey enthusiastically led me into her room to show me a much improved attempt. Again, I praised her and suggested a final improvement, that she place the pillow on the bed the next time. On the third morning, she excitedly showed me a well-made bed! Of course, I praised her fine job and told her how proud I was that she had tried so hard and stuck with it. She now makes her bed every morning without prompting and even often criticizes my own bed-making skills.

At other times, parents may find that they need to reinforce the *absence* of a negative behavior. In other words, if a child is exhibiting an inappropriate behavior, parents may need to praise the child for *not* doing the behavior. Again, Lindsey thoughtfully provides another example.

Most parents of young children are all too familiar with how they tend to pester you when you are on the telephone. Lindsey was no exception. The more I told her to wait until I got off the phone, the more the behavior persisted. It wasn't too long before I realized that I was rewarding her negative behavior with my attention and needed to make a change.

Parents may find that they need to reinforce the *absence* of a negative behavior. In other words, if a child is exhibiting an inappropriate behavior, parents may need to praise the child for *not* doing the behavior.

Within the next several days a wonderful opportunity presented itself. One evening, the telephone rang, and as I answered it I noticed that Lindsey was playing with some toys nearby. The call turned out to be a wrong number, and since I was only on the telephone a short time, Lindsey did not have sufficient time to react. I immediately seized the opportunity to tell her how much I appreciated her letting me speak on the phone unmolested. She initially appeared surprised, but it was only a few seconds before a bright smile lit her young face, as if she were saying "Yeah, I guess I did do that, didn't I?"

Later that same evening, the telephone rang again. As I went to answer it, I heard Lindsey running down the hall behind me. Much to my surprise, she placed her head on my lap and kept it there for the entire forty-five-minute conversation. When I hung up, she immediately raised her head and blurted, "Daddy, aren't you proud of me? I didn't bother you while you were on the phone!" I picked her up, hugged her, and told her that I was indeed very pleased with her. I made a big deal of her accomplishment, and she has not bothered me while I have been on the telephone since. I still try to remember to praise her occasionally for acting appropriately while I am on the phone.

Making it easier for a child to receive parental attention by behaving appropriately is the most effective way to increase desirable behaviors and decrease undesirable ones. It simply works better than paying attention to children only when they misbehave. This approach also has the added advantage of increasing a child's sense of competence, confidence, and self-esteem. It also increases a child's *motivation* to do well.

If a child brings home a report card with four A's and one C, the parents can choose to focus on either the A's or the C. Attending primarily to the C increases the child's sense of shame and failure. It does little to motivate that child to work harder during the next grading period.

DAD: Let me have a look at your report card, Son.

SON: [handing him the report card] OK, Dad. See, I got A's in everything but math.

DAD: Yes, but you got a C in math. Didn't I tell you that you need to do your homework every night? If you'd pay more attention to your homework and spend less time playing video games, you'd make an A in math, too.

SON: But, Dad. . . .

DAD: I don't want to hear anything else about it. There are going to be some changes around here, starting with no more video games until you get that grade up. Do you understand me, Son?

SON: Yes, Dad.

A more effective approach would be for this father to re-inforce the boy's effort and success in obtaining four out of five A's, then follow up with his son and ask whether any assistance is needed with his math class. His son will feel more empowered and more motivated. The chances are good that he will work to bring up the C (because of all the great attention the A's received) and will be more likely to ask for any needed help.

DAD: Let me have a look at your report card, Son.

SON: [handing him the report card] OK, Dad. See, I got A's in everything but math.

DAD: You sure did. It looks like your brought up both your English and your history grade. I'm really proud of you.

SON: [smiles] Thanks, Dad.

DAD: It looks like you had a little trouble in math. Anything I can do to help?

SON: I don't think so. I just got a little behind when we studied long division. I ended up blowing a couple of quizzes.

DAD: Do you think you have a handle on it now?

SON: Well . . . I think so, but I'm not really sure.

DAD: Tell you what. Why don't I give you a little extra help after school next week, and we'll see if we can't get that grade up a bit.

SON: [relieved] Thanks, Dad, that would be great.

Sometimes it may seem quite difficult to find behavior that can be rewarded, especially with toddlers. A woman who had just heard me speak at a local PTA meeting came up to me afterward to ask about her child. "I'm trying to potty train my daughter. How on earth am I supposed to reward behavior that she isn't even doing?"

I acknowledged that potty training can be a difficult and challenging time. I suggested that she take her daughter to the bathroom with her every time that she went herself. Sit her on her training toilet and talk to her as she normally would. Eventually, the little girl will go herself, either because she will follow her mother's example or perhaps just because of random chance. When she finally goes, the mother can make a big deal out of her accomplishment. I reminded her to be patient in her attempt to "catch her being good."

As a parent, you have the ability to choose whether to focus on and reward your child's positive behavior or to dwell primarily on negative behavior.

Things to Remember

Requiring Children to Misbehave

- All children want attention.
- Reward children with praise for positive behaviors rather than negative behaviors.
- Reward specific behaviors rather than giving general praise.
- Try to "catch" children behaving, and reward them for that behavior.
- Break desired behaviors into smaller steps, commending each step.
- Sometimes it may be necessary to reward the absence of a negative behavior.

Again, the most important thing to remember is that children want attention; attention is rewarding. As a parent, you have the ability to choose whether to focus on and reward your child's positive behavior or to dwell primarily on negative behavior. It may take some initial effort to refocus your attention, but the effort will pay big dividends in terms of increased compliance and a happier, healthier child.

Self-Test 2

1. Which of the following is a fundamental parenting truth?
   A. All children want to be punished.
   B. Most parents are far too lenient.
   C. All children want attention.
   D. Most parents are far too strict.

2. Children would rather experience "negative" attention than experience no attention at all.
   True   False

3. Parents need to try to catch their children behaving appropriately and reward them with:
   A. Attention and praise.
   B. Money.
   C. Criticism.

4. Parental praise needs to be focused on _____ behaviors rather than more global positive statements.

5. If a child does not have the skills or knowledge required to perform a specific task, parents may need to:
   A. Seek psychotherapy.
   B. Keep pushing until the child gets it right.

    C. Point out the child's mistakes and provide additional information.

    D. Break the task into smaller, more manageable steps.

6. Sam has an annoying habit of making odd noises at the dinner table. His parents would very much like him to stop this behavior. Sam's parents should:

    A. Point out the behavior when it occurs and politely ask Sam to stop.

    B. Ignore the behavior.

    C. Catch Sam not making the noise and praise him.

    D. Punish Sam by making him leave the table each time the noise is made.

7. A child brings home a report card with several A's, one B, and one C. The parents should react by:

    A. Praising the effort put in on the A's and asking whether the child needs any help with the B or the C subject.

    B. Make the child do extra homework to get the B and C up.

    C. Punish the child for getting a C.

    D. Do nothing.

Self-Test Answers

1. Which of the following is a fundamental parenting truth?

    Answer C: Children will take any type of attention, but positive attention is the most motivating.

2. Children would rather experience "negative" attention than experience no attention at all.

    Answer: True. As strange as it may seem, most children would rather have their parents yelling at them than ignoring them.

3. Parents need to try to catch their children behaving appropriately and reward them with:

Answer A: Children have a tremendous need to please their parents and have their parents demonstrate that approval.

4. Parental praise needs to be focused on_____ behaviors rather than more global positive statements.

   Answer: Specific. Praising a child for a specific positive behavior is much more effective than more general statements such as "You were really good today."

5. If a child does not have the skills or knowledge required to perform a specific task, parents may need to:

   Answer D: Breaking a difficult task into smaller parts increases the chances of success by providing additional opportunities for praise.

6. Sam has an annoying habit of making odd noises at the dinner table. His parents would very much like him to stop this behavior. Sam's parents should:

   Answer C: Sam's parents should make it easier to get their positive attention when he behaves appropriately rather than when he behaves inappropriately.

7. A child brings home a report card with several A's, one B, and one C. The parents should react by:

   Answer A: Again, if praised for putting effort into A's, a child is more likely to try harder. Remember, the good behavior gets the positive attention.

Being Inconsistent

Being inconsistent is one of the most common parenting traps. Not surprisingly, parents offer a multitude of reasons to explain why they are not more consistent with their children, including time pressures, distractions, stress, or simple inattention. Whatever the reason, not providing structure and consistency can contribute to a variety of behavioral problems.

My clients frequently ask me whether it is better for parents to take a strict or a more liberal approach with their children. In fact, good kids are raised in both homes that are authoritarian and ones that are liberal. The most important factor is whether the stated rules are predictable and enforced consistently.

Being consistent means following through on rules and consequences. If you make a rule or threaten to impose a consequence, follow through with what was said. Children quickly learn to test the limits, especially if parents make pronouncements and fail to carry them out.

One beleaguered mother anxiously recounted a recent event involving her fourteen-year-old son, James. James had been told that he needed to clean his room before he would be allowed to go outside and skate with his friends. After completing only part of the job, James started to head out the front door. His mother intercepted him, telling him that he needed to finish cleaning his room before going outside. James defiantly stated that he was going to skate now and that he would finish cleaning his room later. His mother met this challenge by telling him that if he went out the door he would be grounded for the weekend.

Being consistent means following through on rules and consequences. If you make a rule or threaten to impose a conse-quence, *follow through* with what was said.

As James continued to threaten to walk out the door, his mother said, "Don't you go out that door, I mean it!" Each time she made this statement her voice got louder and an-grier. By the time she made the sixth threat, James backed down and returned to the task of cleaning his room.

So what really happened during this exchange between James and his mother? On the positive side, James eventu-ally cleaned his room. Unfortunately, he probably learned some not-so-positive lessons as well.

By telling James that he had better not go out the door five or six times, his mother communicated to James that the first four or five warnings did not matter. He probably al-ready knew that his mother would not follow through unless she was really angry, which he could surmise by the tone of her voice. Because James did not believe that his mother would follow through on her threat after the first warning, he felt free to challenge her until they were both embroiled in an emotionally exhausting scene.

I suspect that James's mother had not been very consistent about following through in the past. I also suspect that if she had made a habit to give only one warning and then immediately followed through with the stated consequence, this negative situation would not have occurred at all. James would have realized that a consequence would have followed the first warning, and he would have had little motivation to keep escalating the situation.

It is equally important for parents to be consistent about rewards and promises. Two young parents came to my office recently complaining that their eight-year-old son did not do his chores. As a result, we designed an incentive system that involved a chart listing his daily chores. Each time he completed a specified chore, his parents placed a sticker on the chart. At the end of the week they counted the number of stickers, and he was able to "cash them in" for various prized activities such as staying up later or having a friend spend the night.

After several weeks, the parents returned to my office complaining that the chart was no longer working, that their son had again begun to neglect his chores. After speaking with the young man, I learned that his parents were not following through with the promised incentives. And the parents were surprised that the system was losing its effectiveness!

By being inconsistent, these parents were not only undermining the chart system but also teaching their son a lesson. They were unintentionally communicating to him that their promises to him were not worth a great deal.

Another family reported frequent battles with their thirteen-year-old daughter, Amy, over doing her homework. After school, Amy wanted to play outside or watch television. Her mother would, at times, insist that she begin her homework as soon as she got home from school. Amy would often protest and whine, which sometimes caused her mother to relent and let her put off doing her homework. As her well-meaning mother put it, "Sometimes it was just too much trouble to argue with her about it."

Amy's conflict with her mother over her homework grew worse, with the arguments arising daily. Amy, not knowing whether her mother would relent on a given day, felt compelled to test her to see what the rules were on that particular afternoon.

These constant conflicts improved only after Amy's mother made her expectations clear to Amy. She told her daughter that she could go outside and play only after she had completed her homework each afternoon. Of course, Amy tested her mother for the first few days after the new rules were outlined, but her mother stuck by her guns. After the first week, Amy came to realize that her mother was not going to give in and quit testing her. The problem was resolved because her mother made her expectations clear and consistently enforced them.

A consistent structure provides a child with a sense of security, predictability, and control. Children are not forced to search for parental boundaries by testing the limits with their behavior.

When parents are consistent and follow through on what they say, it provides a much needed structure that children crave. A consistent structure provides a child with a sense of security, predictability, and control. Children are not forced to search for parental boundaries by testing the limits with their behavior. They can relax and operate within a familiar framework of rewards and consequences. It also teaches them the importance of keeping promises and following through on commitments.

Consistent Routines

Providing consistency and structure also helps with one of the most frequently reported problem areas, morning and bedtime routines. Parents almost universally report that getting a child up and ready for school or prepared for bed is stressful for parents and children alike.

It may sound somewhat mundane, but doing the same tasks at the same times each morning or evening reduces the stress of arguing with, pushing, or cajoling our kids to get dressed, eat, or shower. This structure provides a comfortable predictability that helps prevent each of these routine occurrences from degenerating into a power struggle between parent and child.

After learning this lesson over time, I am happy to say that Lindsey and I rarely argue about either the morning or bedtime routine. This lack of conflict stems directly from the routine that she and I have established over the years.

Each morning, I awaken Lindsey and get into the shower. While I am showering, she gets dressed and does her morning chores (make her bed, feed the dog). I then make breakfast, and we sit down and eat together before I take her to school.

Similarly, our evening routine is just as consistent. Lindsey does her homework while I prepare dinner. We then eat together and talk about the day. While I do the dishes, she finishes her homework and goes upstairs to take her shower, brush her teeth, and get into her pajamas. I then check her homework and spend some quiet time with her reading a book, playing a game, or just talking.

Now this routine may seem very boring to someone who has no children. But to a parent, not having to battle over each step is a real blessing. Because our routine is well established, there is little reason for conflict. Establishing a similar routine for your children will take some initial, up-front effort. Sit down with your children and discuss the newly planned routine. Be upbeat and positive about it and enlist their support. After discussing the routine with your kids, start it the very next day and *follow through!*

Of course, it won't be possible to rigidly adhere to the routine each and every day. Things do come up. However, it is important to stick to it as closely as possible to give your children that all-important sense of security that a well-established morning or evening routine can provide.

If you become aware that the routine for a given evening is going to have to change, forewarn your child about the change whenever possible. Predicting the change for your child helps them understand the change and better cope with it. For example, if you learn that you will have to be at work early for an appointment, sit down and discuss the change with your children the night before. Tell them that they will be getting up at 6:00 instead of 6:30. Let them know that their help in getting ready as quickly as possible is important and will be greatly appreciated. Don't forget to praise their cooperation the following day. You'll be sowing healthy seeds for when the next inevitable exception to the regular routine occurs.

Consistent Discipline

Another area in which consistency is critical involves the application of discipline. Many parents become angry over a child's misbehavior and are good about setting immediate consequences. Perhaps because they are angry, however, they set a harsh or prolonged consequence that is difficult to enforce.

One father would become so angry each time that his son got into trouble at school that he would ground him for the following month. Although at the time he set the consequence he fully intended to see it through, in reality it was difficult or impossible to enforce. In the span of one month, numerous "exceptions" would arise and the restriction would become meaningless. It is far better to set a shorter consequence that is consistently enforced than to set one that is impossible to complete.

Parents should also be aware that it is very important for both parents to agree on rules and consequences and to enforce them consistently. Often, creative children will attempt to "split" the parents by playing one against the other. Parents need to discuss points of disagreement away from the children and come up with a compromise that they both feel comfortable enforcing.

> Parents should also be aware that it is very important for both parents to agree on rules and consequences and to enforce them consistently.

Frequently, parents come to my office with just such a problem. Tom and Cindy had disagreed about discipline for years. Raising their older son had often caused angry and contentious fights between them, but somehow they had muddled through. Now the parents of a precocious five-year-old, they came to me seeking help to heal their differences.

Tom had been raised in a household that was very structured and strict. Spanking was the primary method of discipline. Tom believed firmly in this parenting style and felt that Cindy was much too lax. On the other hand, Cindy did not believe in striking a child and thought that Tom was far too harsh and critical.

Tom was able to reluctantly admit that spanking did not seem to be working as well with their five-year-old as it had with their older son. In fact, the boy just seemed to become more defiant when corporal punishment was used (remember, children want attention, even negative attention, such as spanking).

Being a logical man, Tom was not willing to give up his belief in the parenting style with which he had been raised, but he was interested in trying an experiment. I suggested that they should try some of the techniques explained in this book for one month. They would consciously try to catch their son being good and praise those behaviors. When they needed to discipline, they would give one warning and then institute a consequence such as taking away television time or restricting him from his video games.

At the end of the month, Tom admitted that the new parenting techniques had worked well. Not only had the behavior of his son improved, but Tom got to enjoy his young son more and didn't fight with his wife (I had also quietly suggested to Cindy that she reward Tom's behavior when he used the new parenting techniques).

If you and your spouse disagree on parenting strategies, perhaps suggesting "an experiment" might help, as it did with Tom and Cindy. Keep in mind that one partner may be reluctant to give up his or her style because he or she feels that by doing so they will be admitting that he or she is wrong. To avoid this power struggle, read a parenting book together (I recommend this one), take a parenting class, or even seek the help of a family therapist. Learning then applying new information is often easier if it comes from outside the family.

Presenting a united front and being consistent are so important because, if children feel confident that parental rules are unchanging and consistently enforced, they will not be as prone to test the limits to determine what the rules are this week. Also, if consequences are enforceable and consistently applied, children will be less likely to try to "get away with" a misbehavior.

Conclusion

Consistency is an important way to help your child develop a sense of safety and security, not just in the area of structure and discipline. It is hard to overestimate the value to a child of having a parent consistently inquire about the day at school. Consistently going to sporting events or school functions communicates volumes to a child about the value that child has in his or her parent's eyes. Consistently communicating unconditional love to your children will empower them and reduce unnecessary fear and insecurity.

Despite its obvious advantages, being consistent can be one of the most formidable parenting challenges. Given our hectic lives, providing structure and predictability can be a daunting task. Also, we all have understandable emotional swings. It can be difficult to issue a warning and consequence calmly to your child if you are angry about not getting that promised promotion or if the muffler just decided to abruptly end its relationship with your car.

Despite its obvious advantages, being consistent can be one of the most formidable parenting challenges. Given our hectic lives, providing structure and predictability can be a daunting task.

All I can suggest is to give it an honest and sincere effort. If you slip now and then, don't be too hard on yourself. After all, human beings make mistakes; it's a normal and natural part of life (see mental mine 5). If you do your best to be consistent, it won't be long before you discover that the advantages more than justify the effort.

Things to Remember

Being Inconsistent

- Being strict or liberal does not matter as much as consistently enforcing rules and consequences.
- Follow through each and every time.
- Give one warning and then follow through with the appropriate consequence.
- Consistent rules provide structure that children need for a sense of security, predictability, and control.
- Develop a consistent morning and evening routine.
- Use short and enforceable consequences.
- Don't discipline when angry.
- Parents should present a united front.

Self-Test 3

1. Being consistent means _____ rules and conse-
   quences.
   A. Avoiding
   B. Following through on
   C. Designing effective
   D. Designing harsh

2. How many warnings should a parent give before following
   through with a stated consequence?
   A. Two
   B. None
   C. Three
   D. One

3. Consistent _____ provides children with a sense of
   security, predictability, and control.
   A. Structure
   B. Praise
   C. Punishment
   D. Exercise

4. Which of the following is generally the most effective in con-
   trolling problem behavior?
   A. Longer consequences
   B. Verbal tongue-lashing
   C. Shorter, more intense consequences
   D. Ignoring the behavior

5. Will children attempt to "test the limits" when the rules are in-
   consistent?
   A. Never
   B. Sometimes
   C. Almost always

6. If parents disagree on a particular point, they should:
   A. Discuss it as it comes up so the children will see how dis-agreements are resolved.
   B. Support each other in front of the children and discuss dis-agreements later.
   C. Let the children decide the point.
   D. Contact a morning radio call-in show.

Self-Test Answers

1. Being consistent means _____ rules and conse-quences.

   Answer B: If you say it, do it!

2. How many warnings should a parent give before following through with a stated consequence?

   Answer D: If Parents give one warning, and follow through with appropriate consequences each and every time, further warnings will be unnecessary.

3. Consistent _____ provides children with a sense of se-curity, predictability, and control.

   Answer A: If a child knows what to expect, he or she will not have to test the limits to discover where the boundaries and ex-pectations rest.

4. Which of the following is generally the most effective in con-trolling problem behavior?

   Answer C: Shorter, more enforceable consequences are gener-ally more effective than longer ones during which exceptions are likely to be made.

5. Will children attempt to "test the limits" when the rules are in-consistent?

Answer: Yes. If children are unclear about behavioral boundaries, they will almost always test the limits to determine what they can get away with.

6. If parents disagree on a particular point, they should:

   Answer B: Parents should always strive to present a united front.

Closing the Door on Open Communication

Being able to communicate with our children is probably the most important parenting skill. If children think that they can speak with their parents about how they feel, they feel validated and in control. Effective communication is essential in teaching children to value themselves, solve problems, and get along with others.

Communication is also critically important because, as children get older, direct parental control over them significantly decreases. As parents lose the ability to directly influence their children's immediate environment, an open and honest dialogue becomes our most effective, and often only, tool. If a teenager can talk to his or her parents about relationships, drugs, or sex, he or she stands a much better chance of successfully weathering these often turbulent years. Without the ability to communicate effectively, parents will likely be caught up in endless power struggles or forced simply to sit back and "hope for the best."

Communication with children can be either open or closed. All too often parents inadvertently shut down two-way communication with a child. Sometimes parents feel

uncomfortable with the strong emotions with which children expect
them to deal. Other times, in
their desire to teach children,
they may give them advice
that they may not need or
want. In the process, children
will feel as if they have not really been heard and will be
less likely to approach a parent
in the future.

For communication with children to be open and effective, they
must feel that parents are willing to
truly hear them with their full and honest attention. If they
fear that an attempt to speak with a parent will trigger a
tirade or a torrent of well-rehearsed criticism, they will simply quit trying to communicate.

One way to create closed communication is to respond to
children or teenagers using one of the following roles.

> For communica-
> tion with children
> to be open and
> effective, children
> must feel that
> parents are willing
> to truly hear them
> with their full
> and honest
> attention.

The Authoritarian Parent

A parent employing this communication style is very concerned with maintaining control. Since strong feelings are so
"untidy," this parent will order the child to "shape up and fly
right." Using orders, demands, or threats, the Authoritarian
Parent tells the child simply to get rid of what they perceive
to be unnecessary or unwanted feelings. This parent may
make statements like the following:

"Take it easy—there's no need to cry."
"You don't need to feel like that."
"Don't you dare raise your voice to me!"

Authoritarian parents frequently interrupt and override their children.

MOTHER: Young lady, get in here and help me with the dishes!
DAUGHTER: But Mom, I'm right in the middle of a math problem. Can't I finish it first?
MOTHER: I don't care what you're in the middle of. I told you to get in here and help me right this minute!

This communication style clearly indicates that the parent puts little value in what the child is feeling, thinking, or doing. It operates on the premise that the parent, who is larger, stronger, and smarter, has more important needs than does the child. It minimizes the child's needs and conveys the message that the parent is not interested in anything that the child has to say.

The Lecturing Parent

Any parent who has fallen into using this communication style has seen his or her child's eyes glaze over or roll upward as the psychological shields go up. This parent tends to shut down communication by immediately launching into a lecture. The favorite word employed by the Lecturing Parent is *should*. Having only the *correct* feelings is this parent's major concern. Some statements that might be employed by the Lecturing Parent could be these:

"You shouldn't get so upset. Your teacher knows what is best for you."
"You shouldn't feel that way—you know that's not what I meant."
"You shouldn't be so bored—it's a beautiful day!"

This communication style also closes communication between parent and child because the child, in essence, is being told what he or she should feel and do.

SON: Mom, I called Tony and asked him to come over. He said he was too busy again. That's the third time. I don't think Tony likes me anymore.

MOTHER: Well, you shouldn't be calling that Tony anyway. I told you that he's just not the kind of boy you should be spending time with. You should call Frank, down the street. Now that's someone you should be calling.

SON: Oh, Mom. . . .

Like the son in this example, no one likes to be told what to do or how they should feel. And no one likes to be constantly on the receiving end of a lecture.

The Blaming Parent

This parent is very concerned with letting a child know how superior the parent is. The primary goal seems to be to make the child understand that the parent is older, wiser, and always correct. A Blaming Parent might make these kinds of statements:

"What did I tell you? I knew that this was going to happen."
"If you had just listened to me. . . ."
"See what I mean?"

At times, a Blaming Parent may choose to use sarcasm, name-calling, and put-downs to make his or her point. These destructive techniques not only make this parent seem superior, but also belittle the child. Some examples might include the following:

"You can be so stupid."
"What have you gone and done this time?"
"Don't be an idiot. That will never work."

Children of parents who use the blaming style of communication become hesitant to discuss anything with their parents. They learn that whatever they do, it just won't be good enough.

Children of parents who use the blaming style of communication become hesitant to discuss anything with their parents. They learn that whatever they do, it just won't be good enough.

SON: Dad, come see the project that I made for the science fair. It's a solar-powered steam engine. See, when the sunlamp is turned on the oil can, the water begins to heat up and. . . .

DAD: What's wrong with you, boy? That contraption will never work. Look here, you've got the lamp much too far from the can. The water will never get hot enough to generate steam. I swear, sometimes I wonder if you ever take the time to stop and think about what you're doing.

The father in this example totally ignored his son's initiative in designing a project at all. Instead of praising his effort and then communicating with him about possible improvements, he simply shamed his son for doing a less-than-perfect job.

The "There-There" Parent

This parent, for whatever reason, feels as though some quick reassurance will fix any problem. The "There-There" Parent may be afraid of emotional involvement or may be too preoccupied with other things. Unfortunately, this communication style tends to make both children and teens feel as though a parent has not really listened to their feelings or that the parent simply does not care or understand. Some common statements made by the "There-There" Parent are as follows:

"It's no big deal; just shake it off."
"Things will look better tomorrow."
"It's just a phase. It will pass."

DAUGHTER: Dad, I don't know if I want to play basketball anymore.

DAD: Well, why not, honey? The season is almost half over.

DAUGHTER: It's just that every time I get the ball I get it taken away from me. And I never make my free-throws.

DAD: Don't worry about it, honey. I'm sure you'll improve with time.

Although this interchange seems rather harmless on the surface, this well-intentioned father is dismissing his daughter's concerns about her performance. Communication would have been greatly enhanced if he had acknowledged his daughter's fears and concerns before rushing to reassure her that everything will be all right.

Most parents will occasionally slip into one or more of these roles; no one is immune. However, it is important to recognize that each of these roles tends to shut down communication. Avoid using them whenever possible.

The Art of Listening

To have open communication with their children, parents must learn to be good listeners. Being a good listener is not a passive activity but a very active one. As strange as it may sound, listening well takes some concentrated effort. The first step involves making it clear that parents are really available to listen.

Michael, a new client, came into my office to discuss his frustrations with his parents. At age fifteen, he was learning to be more independent, but he still needed occasional guidance and reassurance from his parents. During our initial therapy session, he explained the problem.

"My parents are OK, I guess. I mean, they say all the right things. They tell me that if I ever have problems to come talk to them. The problem is that they don't seem to really mean it. My dad only half-listens. I can tell he doesn't really want to deal with it. He'd rather just go back to his computer. Mom says I can talk to her, too, but all she does is lecture me."

Although Michael's parents honestly thought that they were making themselves available to him, that was clearly not the message that Michael was receiving. Even though his parents said that they were willing to communicate with him, their actions told him that they were unavailable.

I learned a similar lesson when Lindsey was only three years old. At the end of a long day I would come home from work and try to watch the news on television. I really wanted that thirty minutes to unwind from work before beginning our evening together. Lindsey, however, had other ideas. As soon as I got home, she wanted to talk to me and play. From her point of view, I had been gone all day and it was time to play!

The more I put her off, the more insistent and whiny she became. I found that I was not being very successful at either watching the news or playing with my daughter. I was becoming short with Lindsey and unable to enjoy the news. At that point I realized a change in tactics was in order.

Instead of passively listening to Lindsey while I also tried to watch television, I elected to forgo the news and *actively* listen to and play with her. That first few minutes after I arrived home became rich with block play, games of fancy, and stories about her day. I was able to watch her eyes light up and listen to her little-girl laughter. I was happier, she was much happier, and the news still came on at 10 o'clock!

Making a conscious decision to be an active instead of a passive listener in my child's life has affected us greatly throughout the intervening years. Lindsey has not hesitated to discuss with me her trials at school, problems with which she needs help, and even her first boyfriend. I hope that, as she grows into her teenage years, she will still feel as free to share her life joys and concerns with her father as she does now.

Given the daily stress and pressure parents experience in their daily lives, it is easy to dismiss a child or only passively listen to them. Even if a parent is unable to give a child or teen full attention at a particular moment, it only takes a few seconds to stop and respond to them directly. It is much better to tell a child "Honey, Mom's busy right now. Can we talk in fifteen minutes?" than to only half-listen. At least the child will know that her mother or father cares about what she has to say and is willing to make time for her later. If a child is successful at waiting the suggested time, be *sure* to tell her how much you appreciate her patience! Give children the same respect you would expect a spouse or friend to give to you under the same circumstances.

Reflective Listening

Once children know that parents are available to listen to them, they will be more likely to initiate the communication process. Then comes the next step in open communication, *reflective listening*.

Reflective listening acknowledges the fact that everyone communicates on two levels: the content level and the emotional level. The content level of any communication is the actual subject matter involved. The emotional level entails the underlying emotions associated with the content.

Especially with children, who often have a difficult time identifying and verbalizing emotions, acknowledging the emotional content of a conversation becomes a critical listening skill.

When parents acknowledge the emotional content in their children's messages, they're letting them know that they have been heard, that the parents have been actively listening. If children feel that they have been heard and understood, they will feel validated and be more likely to continue the conversation. Reflective listening promotes and sustains open communication.

Reflective listening acknowledges the fact that everyone communicates on two levels: the content level and the emotional level.

Specifically, reflective listening involves trying to understand the emotional content of the message and then reflecting it back to the child. Notice how the communication is stopped short when only the content of the message is addressed.

JILL: My teacher wouldn't let me turn in my homework just because it was one day late!

PARENT: Well, you would have had the homework in on time if you had gotten off the telephone at a decent hour.

JILL: Yeah, I guess so.

SAM: Mom, Johnny went off to play with the new kid at recess today. I had to play by myself.

MOTHER: Don't worry. You've got lots of other friends.

SAM: Sure, Mom.

It's easy to see how addressing only the content in these dialogues did not encourage the children to continue to talk to their parents. In fact, the children immediately sensed that their parents didn't understand what they were trying to communicate. When these parents neglected to address the underlying emotions in the messages, effective communication was stopped cold. Jill was not given a chance to talk about how she really felt, and Sam was given the message that his feelings were not appropriate.

Now notice the dramatic difference in these parent-child communications when the parents make a determined effort to respond to the emotions as well as the specific content of what is being said:

JILL: My teacher wouldn't let me turn in my homework just because it was one day late!

PARENT: That sounds frustrating.

JILL: Yeah, I guess so, but I was mostly embarrassed. She said it loud enough for the whole class to hear.

PARENT: I can see how that would be embarrassing.

SAM: Mom, Johnny went off to play with that new kid at recess today. I had to play all by myself.

MOTHER: I bet that hurt your feelings.

SAM: It sure did!

In both of these examples, the parent tried to identify and reflect a feeling back to the child. Since the emotional reflections were stated tentatively, not as a definite statement, Jill was able to adjust her response to reflect more accurately how she really felt. In both examples the exchange led to more open and effective communication.

It is particularly important to pay attention when children express anger. Anger is a sort of "umbrella emotion" under which other emotions lie. When children express anger, they may actually be feeling one of several possible emotions.

For example, seventeen-year-old Shane has just gotten a call from his girlfriend telling him that she does not want to go out with him anymore, that she has found someone else whom she would rather date. As Shane gets off the telephone, he slams down the receiver and lets loose a stream of rather choice words. He kicks a chair and then throws himself down on the sofa, hurling one of the pillows across the room. Shane seems pretty angry, right?

Anger is a sort of "umbrella emotion" under which other emotions lie. When children express anger, they may actually be feeling one of several possible emotions.

On the surface Shane does appear angry. However, I suspect that he is actually feeling something else. It is likely that he is feeling abandoned, rejected, betrayed, afraid, lonely, or some combination of these emotions. Because he hasn't identified what he is feeling yet, he opts for the easiest, broadest, and most accessible emotion—anger.

Now assume his father walked into the room just after Shane threw himself onto the sofa and tossed the pillow. Here's what might happen if his father responded only to Shane's apparent anger:

DAD: Whoa, Son, what on earth has gotten into you? You look like you could chew nails.

SHANE: It's that stupid Sandy. She dumped me. I can't be-
         lieve that she would rather go out with that senior,
         Benjamin. [Shane throws another pillow.]

DAD: Hey, Son, I know you're angry, but you need to set-
         tle down. You'll find another girlfriend. It's her loss,
         right?

SHANE: Damn it, Dad. You just don't understand. [Shane
         storms from the room.]

Because this concerned father didn't look below his son's
surface anger, his son didn't feel as though he was being
heard by his father. Consequently, he leaves the room in a
huff, leaving his father feeling lost and confused. The following example shows how this interchange might have gone if
the father had been sensitive to the emotions underlying his
son's anger:

DAD: Whoa, Son, what on earth has gotten into you? You
         look like you could chew nails.

SHANE: It's that stupid Sandy. She dumped me. I can't be-
         lieve that she would rather go out with that senior,
         Benjamin. [Shane throws another pillow.]

DAD: [Sits down next to his son] Hey, I know that getting
         dumped can feel pretty rough. Kinda makes you
         wonder what's wrong with you, doesn't it?

SHANE: Yeah, I guess it does. I just never expected she
         would do something like that.

DAD: Every time a girl used to give me my walking pa-
         pers I'd usually feel like kicking a hole in the wall.
         Then I'd usually settle down and realize that I was
         really just feeling hurt.

SHANE: It really does hurt.

DAD: [Puts arm around Shane] I know it does, Son. I know it does.

In this second example, the father makes a concerted attempt to see beyond his son's initial burst of anger. He doesn't try to minimize what his son is feeling or make a premature effort to encourage him to get over it. Instead, he simply tries to identify and reflect what his son might be feeling. I suspect Shane will be likely to seek out his father in the future when he is feeling overwhelmed or confused.

In many cases, it may be necessary to reflect *both* the emotions and the content of the message. By addressing both levels, a parent can communicate that he or she is really listening. It also gives the child a chance to correct either the facts or the underlying emotions being conveyed. Again, parents should remember to phrase their responses in a tentative manner. The father in the next example does a good job of addressing both the content and the emotions communicated by his son.

JOSH: That was a dumb birthday party. I wish they hadn't even invited me. Nobody wanted to play with me.
DAD: You felt left out when your friends didn't include you?
JOSH: Well, they let me play, but they weren't very nice to me.
DAD: So your feelings were hurt because they were mean?
JOSH: Uh-huh.

By addressing the emotions and the content, this father allowed Josh to express his feelings and have a chance to clarify the actual events that took place. He paved the way for an open-ended communication on both the emotional and content levels.

Using reflective listening may seem awkward in the beginning. Many parents are not used to having to slow down and think about how to frame a response. It's much easier to just react without thinking. However, like learning any new skill, learning to use reflective listening will become easier with time and practice.

Open and Closed Communication

By being available to communicate with your children and by being a good listener, you can create an atmosphere that promotes the security and trust necessary for truly effective, open communication. Not being readily available or slipping into destructive parenting roles has just the opposite effect. Your children will not feel that they can approach you and be actively heard.

> **B**y being available to communicate with your children and by being a good listener, you can create an atmosphere of security and trust.

Here are some examples to evaluate to see whether you feel that they promote open or closed communication between parent and child. Judge each example based on the parenting styles and the listening techniques discussed in this chapter. After you have jotted down your impressions, read my own to see whether we agree.

Example 1

SONYA: Sorry I'm late, Dad, but you won't believe what happened at school today. Jennifer skipped seventh period and was given detention for a week.

DAD: Well, good! I hope you realize now that Jennifer is a bad influence on you. I'm sure she got just what she deserved.

Was this communication open or closed?
Open_____   Closed_____

Example 2

TODD: Mom, can you make Jason stay out of my room? He messes with my stuff and bothers me while I'm trying to do my homework.

MOM: Well, Todd, why don't you just close the door?

Was this communication open or closed?
Open_____   Closed_____

Example 3

MATT: I don't see why I can't stay out until midnight—all of my friends get to.

DAD: So you feel that it's unfair to have an 11:30 curfew?

Was this communication open or closed?
Open_____   Closed_____

Example 4

MARTHA: I can't believe Stan asked Judy to go to the dance instead of me. I mean, we've gone out three times already.

MOTHER: Don't worry about it, honey. You'll find someone else to go out with.

Was this communication open or closed?
Open_____   Closed_____

Example 5

DAMON: Mom, I really studied for that math test. I don't know what happened. I guess I'm just stupid when it comes to math.

MOM: Sounds like you're frustrated and ready to give up.

DAMON: I sure am, but I don't want to have to go to summer school. Do you think that I could get a tutor?

Was this communication open or closed?
Open_____   Closed_____

My Impressions

Example 1

This communication is unmistakably closed. This parent has fallen into the Blaming Parent role. Because of the judgmental nature of her father's response, Sonya is unlikely to continue the conversation. She will probably hesitate to approach him in the future, too.

Example 2

The Lecturing Parent role adopted by this mother makes this a closed communication. By giving immediate unsolicited advice, she fails to acknowledge this young man's anger and frustration about having his privacy violated.

Example 3

This father's response definitely encourages open communication. He mirrors his son's feelings of unfairness and leaves the door open for further discussion. Even if this father declines to alter the curfew, Matt undoubtedly felt as though his complaint and feelings had been heard and acknowledged.

Example 4

This mother responds to her daughter with the classic "There-There" Parent role. Unfortunately, her response minimizes her daughter's feelings and closes the door on further communication.

Example 5

This mother avoids expressing advice too quickly or glossing over her son's feelings of frustration and disappointment. She not only validates his emotions but allows him an opportunity to work out a solution for himself. This young man will probably feel free to approach his wise mother with future problems.

Nonverbal Communication

Finally, no discussion about effectively communicating with children or teenagers would be complete without some mention about the importance of nonverbal communication. Being sensitive to children's nonverbal cues can tell a parent a great deal about their moods, feelings, and current state of mind. Also, children are extraordinarily sensitive to nonverbal cues from their parents.

> Being sensitive to children's nonverbal cues can tell a parent a great deal about their moods, feelings, and current state of mind. Also, children are extraordinarily sensitive to nonverbal cues from their parents.

As we have discussed, encouraging children to express their emotions is vitally important, and responding to nonverbal behavior offers a wonderful opportunity to do just that. Here are some examples of constructive responses to nonverbal cues:

"The way you are rolling your eyes suggests you don't agree. Am I right?"

"You seem very pleased with yourself." (responding to a smile)

"I see you're frustrated about not getting to play with Jason. Want to talk about it?"

Also important is nonverbal behavior that is exhibited by parents themselves. Nothing will shut down a child's attempt to communicate faster than a parent saying, "I'm listening," when it is clear that he or she is clearly distracted by something else. Here are a few tips to improve your own nonverbal communication with your children:

- Stop what you are doing and give your child your full attention.
- Make good eye contact.
- Lean forward, especially when your child is communicating something that he or she considers to be important.
- Avoid interrupting. Letting your child finish what he or she wants to say communicates caring and sincere interest.
- Nod occasionally.
- Smile when appropriate to let the child know that talking to him or her is not a burden.
- A periodic "Uh-huh" or "Mmm" lets the child know that you are actively listening.

Conclusion

As parents learn to improve their ability to communicate with their children, they will likely notice several important changes. Their children will approach them more readily to discuss their concerns. Because they will feel that they have

Things to Remember

Closing the Door on Open Communication

- As children get older, open communication is a parent's most effective tool.
- Open communication minimizes power struggles between parent and child.
- Give children and teens your full attention when communicating with them.
- There are several parenting styles that promote closed communication:
    Authoritarian Parent
    Lecturing Parent
    Blaming Parent
    "There-There" Parent
- Listening is an *active* process.
- Whenever possible, use reflective listening.

been heard and understood, children will be more compliant with parental suggestions. The children themselves will also learn these communication skills from their parents and will experience less conflict with siblings and peers.

Effective communication becomes even more critical as children get older. Parents will have to rely increasingly on their ability to communicate with their teenagers as their direct control decreases. Practicing good communication skills with younger children gives you a head start on those pesky teenage years.

Self-Test 4

1. As children grow older, what becomes a parent's most effective parenting tool?
   A. Car keys
   B. Taking away privileges
   C. Praise
   D. Communication

2. What sort of process is listening?
   A. Active
   B. Passive

3. *Should* is the favorite word employed by the _____ parent.
   A. Authoritarian
   B. Lecturing
   C. Blaming
   D. "There-There"

4. The _____ parent is primarily concerned with maintaining control.
   A. Authoritarian
   B. Lecturing
   C. Blaming
   D. "There-There"

5. The _____ parent uses quick reassurance to deal with a child's problems or strong feelings.
   A. Authoritarian
   B. Lecturing
   C. Blaming
   D. "There-There"

6. The primary goal of a _____ parent is to make sure the child understands that the parent is older, wiser, and always correct.
   A. Authoritarian

B. Lecturing
C. Blaming
D. "There-There"

7. The two levels of communication are the content and the
   _____ level.

8. This technique is one in which the facts and the emotions of a
   given communication are paraphrased and restated to the
   child.
   A. Unconditional love
   B. Problem solving
   C. Reflective listening
   D. Verbal backhand

Self-Test Answers

1. As children grow older, what becomes a parent's most effective
    parenting tool?

    Answer D: As direct control of children and teens decreases, the
    need to have open communication with them increases.

2. What sort of process is listening?

    Answer A: Listening to children requires much more than sim-
    ply hearing the words.

3. *Should* is the favorite word employed by the _____
    parent.

    Answer B: This word tends to indicate the lecturing style of par-
    enting.

4. The _____ parent is primarily concerned with main-
    taining control.

    Answer A: The authoritarian parenting style is concerned with
    power and dominance.

5. The _____ parent uses quick reassurance to deal with a child's problems or strong feelings.

   Answer D: The "There-There" parenting style tends to invalidate a child's feelings.

6. The primary goal of a _____ parent is to make sure the child understands that the parent is older, wiser, and always correct.

   Answer C: The blaming parenting style often uses name-calling, put-downs, and I-told-you-so's.

7. The two levels of communication are the content and the _____ level.

   Answer: Emotional. In many communications, the underlying emotions are more important than the facts.

8. This technique is one in which the facts and the emotions of a given communication are paraphrased and restated to the child.

   Answer C: Reflective listening helps children feel that they have been heard and understood.

Playing "Fix-It"

No matter how wonderful we are as parents, our children are going to encounter problems, dilemmas, and obstacles. It's an inescapable part of life. It is also quite difficult for most parents to watch their children wrestle with these challenges.

As adults who have been around the block a time or two, parents want to use their considerable life experience to save their children from the pain and discouragement that they have experienced themselves. They naturally want to protect their kids from making mistakes and less-than-ideal choices. In their desire to guide and protect their children, however, many parents fall into the trap of playing "fix-it."

By rushing in to solve problems for our children, we deprive them of the opportunity to learn from the consequences of their actions. We inadvertently encourage them to become dependent on us instead of learning to be independent and self-sufficient. Failing to let children experience the natural consequences of their behavior also promotes frustration and resentment because their natural desire to explore and grow is being restricted.

Teenagers are particularly prone to develop resentment toward or excessive dependence on their parents when parents give advice rather than letting them learn on their own. If parents give advice that turns out well, teenagers are likely to attribute the good outcome to the parents instead of recognizing it as a result of their own action and initiative. Conversely, if parents give advice that doesn't work out, teens are likely to blame the parent for the faulty advice rather than learning from their own mistakes.

> Teenagers are particularly prone to develop resentment toward or excessive dependence on their parents when parents give advice rather than letting them learn on their own.

Raymond's parents made this mistake when he began to have trouble with his soccer coach. One night he came home bitterly complaining to his parents that his coach was not letting him play enough. Meaning well, his father suggested that he speak with his coach about his concerns. Raymond took his father's advice.

The next evening, Raymond came home angry and tearful. His coach had told him that he didn't think that he was concentrating enough in practice and giving his best effort. He told Raymond that he would not get any additional playing time until he saw some improvement in his attitude and effort during practice.

Raymond, of course, came home blaming his father for suggesting that he speak with his coach. By giving him direct advice instead of helping him decide how to solve his own problem, his father had unwittingly created a situation in which Raymond could avoid his own responsibility and instead blame his father for giving poor counsel.

The habit of stepping in to solve problems for children often begins when they are very young. In the bustle of daily activity, it is often more convenient to "just get the job done" rather than take the time to teach the child how to perform the task independently. Diane's situation with her six-year-old son Doug is typical.

"I just can't seem to get him dressed and out the door in the mornings. We are always so rushed for time. Doug will start to get dressed, and then I'll find him sitting in front of the TV. I usually end up putting on his shoes and buttoning his shirt for him just so we can get out the door!"

Can you see the problem with this situation? Little Doug has no motivation to dress himself. His mother will eventually do it for him, *and* he gets to watch cartoons. Why should Doug learn to dress himself?

An approach that will be much more successful in the long term will take a little more initial effort. Diane needs to take the time to restructure the morning routine so that Doug is motivated to dress himself and will experience the logical consequences of his action or inaction.

Diane could sit down with Doug before he goes to bed and calmly state the problem with the morning routine. She could then tell him about the "new rules" that are to begin the next morning. She can then explain that Doug must stay in his room until he is completely dressed, shoes and all. Only then will he be allowed to watch cartoons.

Diane should be very positive as she describes the new system to Doug, expressing her belief that he will be able to dress quickly so that he can go downstairs to watch cartoons. She should help him dress only if he requests help with a specific problem, and even then, she can show him how to do it himself the next time.

With a little planning, Diane can create a situation in which:

1. Doug is rewarded with more cartoon time if he dresses quickly.
2. Doug will lose cartoon time if he chooses to dawdle.
3. Diane has created an opportunity to praise her son and build his self-esteem. Before the "new rules," she was always being critical of his tardiness.
4. Doug learns to be more independent and responsible.

Amy is a ten-year-old in a family with six children. For this rather large family to function effectively, each child is responsible for several chores. Amy's assigned chore is to put the dishes in the dishwasher after they have been cleared from the table and rinsed by her siblings. However, each night her mother has to battle with Amy to get her to put away the dishes. Eventually, her parents grow tired of the battle and help her with her task.

The problem was solved when her parents decided to employ a logical consequence. Since Amy liked to ride her bike after dinner with her friends on the block, her parents employed this activity as an incentive. When Amy completed the loading of the dishwasher, she was allowed to ride her bike. If the job was undone or she argued about it, she was not allowed to go outside that evening. The quicker she did the job, the more time she was able to spend outside. This solution was simple but effective.

Allowing children to experience logical consequences works for kids of all ages, including teenagers. If a teen consistently comes home late for dinner, don't save her a plate.

The logical consequences of her chronic lateness—going hungry or having to fix a meal herself—will teach a much more valuable lesson than will direct parental intervention.

Similarly, if a teen forgets to put his dirty clothes in the hamper to be washed, he will learn from the experience of having no clean clothes to wear to school. It might be an even better practice to make a teen responsible for his own laundry from the beginning. Remember, the foremost parenting goal is to teach children to be independent and responsible adults.

Letting children and teens learn from the consequences of their actions is a valuable parenting tool. However, in some instances the child's safety is an issue, or the child's actions may violate the rights of others in the home. In both of these situations, more direct parental involvement will be required.

For example, safety is an issue if a child wishes to play street hockey on a street that is too busy. The logical consequence of getting hit by a car is not acceptable. Another discipline strategy is required. Similarly, if a teen plays his music so loud that others are disturbed, the rights of others are violated and parental intervention may be necessary.

Problem Solving

In those instances in which a parent needs to play an active role, it is still important to involve the child in the process. This approach is called *problem solving*. When such a situation arises, a parent will be much more effective eliciting the help of the child to solve the problem cooperatively rather than simply handing down orders and directives. This process takes a little more time and effort, but it also decreases the likelihood of a power struggle between parent and child. By involving the child in the process, parents can also assure a much greater degree of cooperation and a sense of accomplishment when the problem is successfully resolved.

Problem solving begins by clearly and calmly stating the problem to be addressed. The particulars should be discussed at a time when emotions are not running high. There should be no accusations or blame, just a simple statement of the problem at hand. For example:

> "Son, I noticed that you left your bicycle behind my car again this morning."
>
> "When you play your music after 10 o'clock, your father and I have a hard time getting to sleep."

The next step involves soliciting a list of possible solutions from the child. Do not judge the solutions as they come up; simply note them or write them down. If your child has difficulty coming up with alternatives, you may have to make some tentative suggestions. Statements such as "Have you considered . . . ?" or "Perhaps we could . . ." often work well.

After all the possible alternatives have been listed, discuss each in turn. When the most promising solution has been selected, make an agreement (verbal or written) to give it a try and then check back in a specified time to see how well it worked.

Here is a possible problem-solving scenario:

Scenario 1

DAD: Eddie, when I left for work today, I noticed that you left your bike behind my car again. I almost ran over it.

EDDIE: I know Dad. I'm sorry.

DAD: I know you're sorry, Son, but since you are having trouble taking care of the problem on your own, I think we need to figure out what to do about it together. Why don't we do that now? Any suggestions?

EDDIE: [Smiling] Well, you could look behind your car before you leave.

DAD: OK, what else?

EDDIE: I could remember to put it in the garage.

DAD: Anything else?

EDDIE: No, I can't think of anything else.

DAD: Well, maybe I could take the bike away for a week or so next time I find it behind the car to remind you to put it away. Or maybe I could just run over it.

EDDIE: I'm not sure I like those choices.

DAD: Let's just see what we've got here. First, I don't think just letting you try to remember is enough. That's what we've been trying, isn't it?

EDDIE: I guess so, yeah. And I really don't want you to run over my bike. I just got it for Christmas.

DAD: Well, maybe we could combine the last two alternatives. You said you think that I should look behind the car before I leave, which I could do. If I find the bike there, I could take it away for a week to remind you to put it away. Sound fair?

EDDIE: How about taking it away for a couple of days instead of a week?

DAD: If you think a couple of days is enough time, we could give it a try. How about getting together again in two weeks and see how it's going?

EDDIE: OK, Dad, thanks.

In this example, the father could easily have gotten angry and blown up at his son. Instead, he engaged his son in a co-operative attempt to solve the problem rather than create a nonproductive power struggle. The son learned cooperation and problem-solving skills and is more likely to comply with the request because he was involved in the solution. This wise father got the bicycle moved from behind his car and avoided an unpleasant confrontation. When the father remembers to check back with his son in two weeks, they can work together to modify the agreement if necessary. If the plan has been successful, this father has a wonderful opportunity to praise his son's responsibility and build his self-esteem.

The following problem-solving situation is another example of constructively involving children in the decision-making process:

Scenario 2

MOTHER: Julie, do you have any homework tonight?

JULIE: [Looking down] Well, we are supposed to do a math worksheet, but I forgot to bring home my folder.

MOTHER: Julie, that's the third time this week you've forgotten to bring home your assignments from school.

JULIE: I know, Mom. I'm sorry.

MOTHER: Well, honey, I think we need to sit down and talk about it. We need to figure out some way to help you remember your assignments. You know if you keep forgetting your homework, it's really going to affect your grades.

JULIE: Yeah, Mom, I know.

MOTHER: Do you have any suggestions?

JULIE: Well, I could try harder to remember.

MOTHER: OK. What else might work?

JULIE: I could call Sally when I get home and get the assignments from her.

MOTHER: That's another idea. I just had a thought. Maybe we could use an assignment sheet. You could write down your assignments and have your teacher initial it after class. Then you could use the sheet at the end of the day to make sure you have all your assignments.

JULIE: Well, I don't know.

MOTHER: Let's see what we've got so far. You suggested trying harder to remember your assignments. Do you think that will work?

JULIE: [Smiling] Well, I guess it hasn't worked too well this week.

MOTHER: Let's see, you also suggested calling Sally every evening. Do you think she might get tired of giving you your assignments every night?

JULIE: Yeah, I guess she probably would.

MOTHER: Well, what do you think of the idea of using an assignment sheet?

JULIE: Mom, I don't want to go up every day and have the teacher sign a sheet. I'd look like a dork!

MOTHER: Tell you what. Why don't we make up an assignment sheet on the computer right now? If you can show me that you can write down your assignments and check it yourself, then you won't have to have the teacher sign it. Let's try it that way for two weeks and see how it goes. What do you think?

JULIE: That sounds like it might work. Thanks, Mom.

In this case, not only did Julie feel that she was a part of the solution, but she also has a strong incentive to make it work (so the teacher won't have to sign her sheet). If this mother is as smart as she appears to be, she will follow up in two weeks and reward her daughter's success with praise or other tangible reinforcement.

Using a problem-solving approach helps alleviate the problem behavior, teaches adaptive coping skills, and increases a child's sense of competence, independence, and responsibility.

So, to avoid the "playing fix-it" parenting trap, it is important to let children experience and learn from the natural and logical consequences of their actions whenever possible. Allowing children to learn from logical consequences is appropriate

Things to Remember
Playing "Fix-It"

- Whenever possible, let children learn from logical consequences.
- Solving problems for children fosters resentment and dependency.
- Letting children learn from logical consequences is *not* appropriate when the child's safety is involved or when the rights of others are violated.
- Use a problem-solving approach when direct parental involvement is necessary.

when personal safety and others' rights are not at issue. When more direct parental involvement is required, using a problem-solving approach helps alleviate the problem behavior, teaches adaptive coping skills, and increases a child's sense of competence, independence, and responsibility.

Self-Test 5

1. By rushing in to "fix" problems, parents may:
   A. Encourage dependence.
   B. Increase frustration.
   C. Promote resentment.
   D. All of the above

2. Which of the following would be a logical consequence of leaving dirty dishes in the sink after the evening meal?
   A. Being grounded for a week
   B. Not getting breakfast until the dishes are done
   C. Losing television-watching privileges
   D. Going to bed an hour early

3. Letting a child experience the logical consequences of his or her behavior may *not* be appropriate when:
   A. The rights of others are being violated.
   B. It is very late at night.
   C. Safety is an issue.
   D. Both A and C

4. Problem solving is often a good technique to use when direct parental involvement is required. The advantages of a problem-solving approach include:
   A. It saves time.
   B. It increases cooperation and decreases power struggles.
   C. It is easier.
   D. Oprah would like it.

5. The first step in problem solving is to clearly and calmly state the situation to be addressed. Which of the following statements best expresses the problem?

   A. "I've told you a million times not to have friends over when your father and I are not at home."

   B. "Your father and I worry about what could happen to you or the house if others are here when we are away."

6. Which of the following statements is true?

   A. Problem-solving alternatives should initially be listed without comment.

   B. Each problem-solving alternative should be judged as it is presented.

Self-Test Answers

1. By rushing in to "fix" problems, parents may:

   Answer D: Remember, the major parenting goal is to teach children to be independent and responsible.

2. Which of the following would be a logical consequence of leaving dirty dishes in the sink after the evening meal?

   Answer B: This action teaches a direct consequence without direct parental intervention.

3. Letting a child experience the logical consequences of his or her behavior may *not* be appropriate when:

   Answer D: Direct parental involvement is probably required when safety and/or the rights of others are involved.

4. Problem solving is often a good technique to use when direct parental involvement is required. The advantages of a problem-solving approach include:

Answer B: Children learn to solve problems constructively and don't feel as though parents are imposing a solution on them. As a bonus, Oprah probably would like this approach.

5. The first step in problem solving is to clearly and calmly state the situation to be addressed. Which of the following statements best expresses the problem?

   Answer B: The second answer clearly states the problem without causing the child to become defensive.

6. Which of the following statements is true?

   Answer A: All ideas and possible solutions should initially be listed without comment.

Us Against Them

A majority of the families that come to my office seeking help have something in common. That is, they have a clear sense that the family is divided along some artificial line. Often this line is drawn between the parents and the children. A pervasive sense exists that "it's us against them."

In any family, it's the parents who have the inherent power in the relationship. This built-in imbalance of power tends to favor a more authoritarian parenting style. In this situation, the children generally become angry, frustrated, and resentful, emotions that usually lead to rebellion and an extended power struggle.

These power struggles can take many forms. Consider Brenda's situation, for example. She had been divorced for two years and was just beginning to date again, which was causing problems for her seven-year-old daughter, Heather. Used to being the center of her attention, Heather began to be uncooperative and throw tantrums when Brenda's boyfriend would come to dinner or take them on an outing. Brenda told Heather in no uncertain terms that she needed to improve her behavior or she would lose some privileges. Despite these consequences, the behaviors persisted.

The Johnsons had a similar problem with their thirteen-year-old son, Jimmy. Mr. Johnson's work required him to travel a great deal, and he would often be out of town for a week or two at a time. Upon his return, he would immediately criticize Jimmy for not keeping his room clean, not cutting the lawn, or leaving clothes around the house. By the time I saw the Johnsons, Mr. Johnson and Jimmy were both visibly resentful and angry, hardly speaking to one another during the initial sessions.

To avoid this split, parents need to adopt a more cooperative parenting style that brings the family together as a team to solve common concerns. Children who are comfortable approaching their parents to get their help in solving problems feel more confident and valued than do children who feel that their parents are inaccessible.

The Family Meeting

One of the most powerful tools that families can employ to promote a more cooperative atmosphere is the *family meeting*. The family meeting is a regularly scheduled gathering in which family members discuss common concerns, including wishes, suggestions, problems, accomplishments, feelings, or questions. Just about any topic is fair game.

Besides allowing family members to address common concerns, a family meeting has other significant advantages. A regularly scheduled meeting gives each family member a sense of power and control. It also fosters a sense of worth because the views and concerns of each family member are heard and valued. It also minimizes discord because family members establish rules in a cooperative manner; each person in the family has input.

When setting up a family meeting, keep in mind several important guidelines:

> One of the most powerful tools that families can employ to promote a more cooperative atmosphere is the *family meeting.*

1. The meeting needs to be held at a regularly scheduled time. Holding the meetings at regular times provides a sense of predictability and consistency. Family members will know that they will have a format each and every week in which to address their concerns. Meetings typically last anywhere from fifteen minutes to one hour.

2. The meeting must be a place where each person can speak openly and honestly, a place to "drop rank." Parents and children should be on as equal a footing as possible. Expressing emotion should not be discouraged as long as it's done appropriately (no name-calling, hitting, etc.). Each person must know that his or her concerns will be heard, *really* heard, even if the desired outcome does not occur.

3. In the meeting, each family member should have an opportunity to speak. Some families choose a different person to run the meeting each week. A child can acquire a wonderful sense of empowerment by being in charge of a weekly meeting, even if some adult assistance is required.

4. As a general rule, it is best to let the children speak first. After their concerns have been heard and addressed, the

parents may take a turn. It is often beneficial for parents first to point out progress on previous meeting topics or praise particularly positive behaviors that have been noted throughout the week before moving on to problematic areas.

5. Agreements that are made in a family meeting should be honored until the next meeting. Changes in agreements will undoubtedly be necessary, but they should only be negotiated within the context of the meeting itself. Statements such as "I know this is important to you, Sally, so why don't we discuss it during our family meeting tomorrow" or "It looks like we do need to modify that rule. Why don't you bring it up Friday at our meeting?" can prevent running conflicts and cut down on bickering during the week.

6. When negotiating an agreement or plan of action, try to get each family member to agree. Voting can create competition and is generally not a good idea. If a consensus cannot be reached, suggest working on something else and discussing the topic at the next meeting. If consensus is still not possible, children should understand that the parent(s) will make the final decision.

When family meetings are first initiated, the children will be unfamiliar with the process and may be reluctant to speak. Parents should not worry if this happens. They should simply encourage the reluctant children to speak when they are ready and move on to parental observations, praise, and concerns. Children will usually warm up to the family meeting idea within a couple of weeks.

Let me illustrate a typical family meeting that was rehearsed in my office several months ago. This family, the

Stedhams, consists of the parents, twelve-year-old Tina, and fifteen-year-old Martin. The Stedhams had been practicing having a family meeting for several weeks and had been trying to negotiate household chores. The meeting begins:

TINA: I want to talk about the chores. I don't think it's fair that I have to rinse the dishes every night and all Martin has to do is put them in the dishwasher.

MARTIN: Yeah, but. . . .

MR. STEDHAM: Martin, please let your sister finish what she wants to say. We'll make sure that you get a chance to speak.

TINA: It's just that washing the dishes is so much harder than putting them away. And by the time I'm through I don't have enough time to do my homework.

MARTIN: Tina's right. By the time we finish the dishes, it's almost time to go to bed. And you two just sit and talk while we work. That's not fair!

MRS. STEDHAM: Let's take one thing at a time, OK? Tina, you think that rinsing the dishes is harder than putting them away, right?

TINA: Yeah!

MRS. STEDHAM: Martin, would you have any objections to switching the rinsing and loading every other night?

MR. STEDHAM: I think that it might be a little difficult to keep track of whose turn it is each night. How about one week rinsing and one week loading?

TINA: Sounds good to me.

MARTIN: That's fine by me, but what about the homework problem and the fact that you guys don't help?

MRS. STEDHAM: Well, I get home the earliest, so I cook the dinner. No one helps me with that.

MR. STEDHAM: Your mother's right—she does end up doing most of the cooking. You guys also have a point about needing more homework time. Tell you what. How about I pitch in with the washing and loading on school nights to help you two get done a little more quickly?

TINA AND MARTIN: All right!

When working with families in conflict, I have often found family meetings to be a wonderful and helpful tool. Children feel more involved in the family decision-making process because their views are heard and valued. Resentment and rebellion decrease because children have a constant format in which to express themselves. During the week, statements like "That would be a good topic to bring up at the next family meeting" help reduce daily conflict. Simply put, a family meeting is a win-win situation for everyone.

Cooperating As a Team

Using a more team-oriented parenting approach has many tangible advantages. Children who feel like a valued member of the "family team" are more likely to be cooperative and assist in solving mutual problems.

Think about how people react in the workplace. Companies that allow employees to have input into important decisions are more efficient. Having to work with an overpowering and unsympathetic boss makes employees feel powerless and resentful. A family works in the same way.

Ms. Foster came into my office with her fifteen-year-old son, Austin. Ms. Foster was a divorced mother with sole responsibility for raising her son. Her former husband was not very good about making his child support payments, and, consequently, finances were tight.

Children who feel like a valued member of the "family team" are more likely to be cooperative and assist in solving mutual problems.

Austin had been getting into minor problems at school. His mother, wanting to be a good parent, tended to yell at him when he misbehaved. They also had frequent arguments about money. Austin would want a new pair of shoes or something that his mother really could not afford. He would keep pressing her about why he couldn't have what he wanted. His mother's anger over the unpaid child support would be triggered, and she would take it out on Austin. Their fights were escalating as this destructive pattern repeated itself.

The secret to helping this family was to get them to change the way they viewed themselves as a family. They both tended to view Ms. Foster as an absolute authority figure and Austin as a wayward child. Austin was becoming frustrated, angry, and bitter while Ms. Foster strongly resented Austin challenging her and making her already difficult life harder.

Things began to change when they started to view themselves as more of a team. As they began to see how mutually dependent they were on one another, they were better able to let go of their respective negative feelings. Ms. Foster sat down with Austin and explained her difficulties with finances and her frustration that she was unable to give him everything that he wanted. Austin was grateful to be included in important family decisions and expressed a desire to continue this process. Their interactions with each other quickly became more positive and mutually supportive.

Parents *do* have the most power within a family. It isn't difficult to use that power to force a child's compliance. However, is teaching our children to comply blindly with authority the ultimate goal? I don't think so. This approach simply breeds resentment and leads to destructive power struggles.

A team-oriented approach to parenting and family life is much more effective. It encourages sensitivity and cooperation. It teaches children to work more effectively with others and helps them feel more powerful, competent, and valued.

The Tindle family discovered the advantages of a team-oriented approach to family problems when Mrs. Tindle decided to go back to school to pursue her degree in accounting. A housewife for many years, Mrs. Tindle understood that her changing role would have significant impact on her husband and their two children.

When she made the decision to return to school, she and her husband sat down and discussed the implications with their children. She told them how she thought she would be happier if she completed her degree. She also discussed the fact that there were going to be some changes in the amount of time that she would be home and that the household routine would be affected.

Mrs. Tindle let her children talk about their fears about her being away from home more often. They discussed the changes in how the kids would get home from school. She asked them to help her with specific chores such as doing the laundry and starting dinner. Finally, she thanked her children for helping her be able to go back to school, telling them that she appreciated their compromises and extra effort. In short, she included them in the process and helped them feel as though they were an important part of the "family team."

Involving the family in impromptu discussions of important issues as they arise is also effective and leads to increased cohesion within the family.

The Tindles also illustrated another important point. Although a regularly scheduled family meeting is a wonderful ideal, less formal team-building approaches are also beneficial. Involving the family in impromptu discussions of important issues as they arise is also effective and leads to increased cohesion within the family.

Teamwork to Overcome Sibling Rivalry

One of the most frequent questions that parents ask me concerns how to cope with sibling rivalry. Some squabbling between siblings is quite natural. Problems seem to arise, however, when the children have different needs that require different parental interventions or the competition between siblings is particularly pronounced. Once again, a team-oriented approach to the problem can be very effective.

The Newsomes have two children. Mark is fourteen and does very well in school. Trey, age nine, has difficulty understanding what he reads. Mrs. Newsome, obviously worried and confused, told me during our first session that Mark complains bitterly about the way she and her husband handle grades. Trey's grades are lower, and frankly, his parents are generally satisfied if he passes his classes. Mark, who doesn't have to contend with Trey's learning difficulties, is expected to meet a higher standard. Mark feels that he is not being treated fairly.

At my suggestion, the Newsomes sat down with Mark and explained the difficulties that Trey experiences with reading comprehension. They were careful not to imply that anything was "wrong" with him, just that it was harder for him through no fault of his own. They told Mark that they needed him to help them make sure that Trey doesn't get

---

Things to Remember

Us Against Them

- A "parents against children" mind-set promotes power struggles and resentment.
- Family meetings can help promote a more cooperative, effective parenting style.
- Family meeting guidelines include these points:
    Family meetings should be held at regularly scheduled times.
    Open communication should be encouraged.
    Everyone in the family should have a chance to speak.
    Children should generally be allowed to speak first.
    Agreements reached at a family meeting are not renegotiated until the next meeting.
    The family should try for consensus on a given issue, but parents should have the final word.

down on himself and feels good about the grades he gets when he is trying his best.

Once included in the solution to this problem, Mark felt himself to be a valued member of the family who had something to contribute to this problem. His sense of unfairness vanished, and he even began to help Trey with his homework!

A cooperative, teambuilding approach definitely takes a little more thought and effort. However, the tremendous rewards make the effort well worth the trouble. Parents will be surprised by the dramatic improvement in attitude and cooperation in their children when a more cooperative parenting approach is used.

Self-Test 6

1. In most families, who has the power in the relationship?
   A. The children
   B. The parents
   C. The grandparents
   D. The family pets

2. A cooperative parenting style promotes feelings of:
   A. Value and confidence.
   B. Blame and shame.
   C. Nausea and congestion.
   D. All of the above

3. A family meeting should be:
   A. At least an hour long.
   B. Held only on the weekend.
   C. Scheduled regularly.
   D. Held only when a problem arises.

4. In a family meeting, who should be encouraged to speak first?
   A. The oldest
   B. Parents
   C. Children
   D. Whoever has the most pressing concern

5. In a family meeting, the expression of emotion should be:
   A. Encouraged
   B. Discouraged

6. Agreements reached in a family meeting should be:
   A. Renegotiated as they arise.
   B. Honored until the next family meeting.
   C. Referred to a radio call-in show.

7. The family meeting should allow each person in the family to be heard. Final decisions are arrived at by:
   A. The parents.
   B. Voting.
   C. A consensus among all family members.
   D. A or C

Self-Test Answers

1. In most families, who has the power in the relationship?

   Answer B: Parents are bigger, stronger, have more experience, and control the money.

2. A cooperative parenting style promotes feelings of:

   Answer A: Children tend to feel like their opinions and feelings will be genuinely heard and that they have some power in the family relationship.

3. A family meeting should be:

   Answer C: Even if the meetings are short, the structure and predictability of a regularly scheduled meeting will pay big dividends.

4. In a family meeting, who should be encouraged to speak first?

   Answer C: Children should be allowed to speak first so that they can express their concerns and emotions without being intimidated by any parental feedback that may have been expressed beforehand.

5. In a family meeting, the expression of emotion should be:

   Answer A: A family meeting is designed to be a safe place for emotions to be expressed.

6. Agreements reached in a family meeting should be:

   Answer B: Agreements may need to be changed, but they should be honored until the next family meeting to prevent strife during the week.

7. The family meeting should allow each person in the family to be heard. Final decisions are arrived at by:

   Answer D: The family should attempt to reach agreements by consensus, but if that is not possible, parents have the final word.

Using "Destructive Discipline"

In every family, parents will find themselves in a situation that demands discipline. As with several other common parenting traps, if parents do not have a plan of action, they can make unnecessary mistakes. These errors can render the discipline attempt less effective and deliver body blows to a child's self-esteem.

Discipline When You Are Not Angry

One of the most destructive mistakes involves attempting to discipline your children when you are angry. Take the case of Jenny and her mother. Jenny's mother had recently divorced and needed to work full-time. Consequently, she expected Jenny to help out with some of the household duties when she got home from school. Jenny agreed to help, but her mother would often find her on the telephone with friends, her chores undone.

Jenny's mother, tired from work and traffic, would become angry and immediately launch into a tirade that quickly escalated into a shouting match. By the time I saw them in my office, they were both very angry and resentful, sitting on opposite ends of my office sofa.

The problem between Jenny and her mother appeared largely to be a matter of timing. Jenny's mother began to anticipate that the chores would not be done when she arrived home. Consequently, she would work up a huge amount of anger before she even walked through the door. Upon finding the chores undone, she immediately exploded, causing Jenny to become defensive and angry.

As an alternative to this destructive pattern, I suggested that her mother assume that the chores would not be completed when she came home from work the next day. If she could accept the fact that they wouldn't be done, she could avoid working up a righteous anger and launching an immediate confrontation. I advised her to bring up the problem *at another time* when they were both calmer and less likely to become defensive. Agreeing, she discussed the problem with Jenny the following weekend.

MOTHER: Jenny, we need to talk about your chores. First, I just want you to understand that I don't want to blow up every time I come home and find that the chores aren't done. When I get angry, it makes me feel bad, and I know you can't like it much either.

JENNY: You do get pretty worked up. I know you work all day and need some help with the chores. I *want* to do them, but I go to school all day and need some time to unwind, too. My friends call and I just get caught up on the phone. Before I know it, you're coming in the front door yelling at me.

MOTHER: I guess I hadn't thought too much about your needing to unwind too. Let's see . . . what if you just took something out of the freezer for dinner and started the laundry? Then you can have some time for yourself. When I get home, we can both start dinner and finish the clothes. What do you think?

JENNY: What about the rest of the chores?

MOTHER: Why don't we just leave those until Saturday morning? We can both get up and get them done quickly if we work together. OK?

JENNY: That sounds great, Mom.

Use Discipline at the Proper Time

Several important factors can determine whether discipline is constructive or destructive. As illustrated with Jenny and her mother, the first is timing. Timing is important because many issues that require discipline make us angry. When tempers flare, the participants raise their "psychological shields" and spend more time defending themselves and counterattacking than in trying to find a workable solution to the problem. If the problem is addressed when emotions are less volatile, a positive

When tempers flare, the participants raise their "psychological shields" and spend more time defending themselves and counterattacking than in trying to find a workable solution to the problem.

outcome is much more likely. By addressing the problem with the chores on the weekend when it was not a hot topic, Jenny and her mother were able to hear and react to each other's concerns. It became much easier for them to arrive at a workable solution.

Although confronting a negative behavior as soon as possible is often best, this approach is not always possible. It is perfectly acceptable to say to a child, "I am very angry right now. I'm going to take some time to calm down and think about this, and we'll talk about it again this evening."

Ann, the mother of a fourteen-year-old, came to my office complaining that her son was beginning to talk back to her every time she attempted to discipline or correct him. After a couple of sessions, the problem became clear: Ann was attempting to correct her son in front of his friends. At age fourteen, her son was becoming increasingly involved with his friends. He wanted to have them over to the house to play video games or to spend the night more than he had when he was younger, a perfectly natural part of being a young teen.

The problem was that Ann would find some chore undone or some clothes on the floor and would immediately run to correct her son. Wanting to save face in front of his friends, he began to argue with her or make a comment under his breath, often to the delight of his buddies!

The problem quickly subsided when Ann learned to wait for a more appropriate time to correct her son. She waited until his friends had left before discussing the problem behavior. She discovered that her son's previous surliness disappeared and he was much more cooperative. Ann had learned the secret of proper timing.

Avoid Name-Calling

Attempting to discipline when you are very angry has other potential drawbacks. In addition to blocking communication and escalating conflict, disciplining when angry can also cause parents to say things that they don't really mean. The damage inflicted by an angry and hurtful statement made in anger can take a very long time to undo.

It's natural to want to strike out with words if you are angry or frustrated, but doing so can have very negative implications for our kids. The Duffys learned this lesson the hard way.

Patrick, age eleven, was constantly bickering with his eight-year-old sister, who would then usually tell their father because she knew that he would intervene. Mr. Duffy, frustrated with the frequency with which these squabbles interrupted his evening, would go running into the room and yell at Patrick. He made loud statements such as, "What's the matter with you, boy? You should know better than to pick on your sister! I've told you a million times to leave her alone. What, are you stupid?"

Mr. Duffy's remarks came back to haunt him a couple of years later when Patrick's grades began to fall. When his father confronted him, Patrick replied, "Well, you always told me I was stupid, so what's the big surprise?"

Mr. Duffy's comments probably had little to do with Patrick's temporary drop in grades. However, Patrick's reply certainly indicated that he had been carrying his father's label around with him for years. When children hear negative labels enough times, they begin to believe them.

I'm no longer surprised by the number of adults that I see in my practice who continue to carry around labels their parents applied to them when they were children. Even years later, adults are still affected by names such as stupid, fat, ugly, or lazy that their parents called them when they were kids. Deep down, they carry these negative labels, often without consciously knowing where they came from.

Set Enforceable Punishments

When angry, parents are more likely to give punishments to their children that are far too harsh and difficult to enforce. I see a number of children who basically laugh at their parents' punishments because they know that there is no way they will stick with them. Jessica is a good example.

Jessica's mother put a premium on academic achievement. She felt that nothing less than an A was acceptable. Problems frequently arose because Jessica was generally an A and B student. When she brought home a B on her report card, Jessica's mother would become angry and ground her for the next six-week grading period.

Jessica never took these restrictions too seriously, because she knew that her mother would eventually weaken and enforce the punishment inconsistently. Dance classes, school functions, and other events would lead her mother to make numerous exceptions, and eventually she would give up altogether—until the next six weeks.

Now, I don't necessarily agree that it is appropriate to ground a child just because she brings a B home from school. However, if her mother really believed restricting her was necessary, she should have given her a shorter, more easily enforced restriction that would not be prone to exceptions. Jessica's mother found it difficult to give the more effective punishment because she always disciplined Jessica for her grades when she was angry. She would have been much better off to let her anger pass and consider an effective intervention when she was calmer.

Give Choices

Another important discipline factor involves giving choices. This approach increases a child's sense of control and lessens the need for a rebellious or confrontational response. If a parent gives a behavioral choice and then disengages from the situation, the child often selects the best alternative.

This typical situation between Mike and his sixteen-year-old son, David, provides a good example of the use of both timing and choices. David has a Saturday midnight curfew for which he was once again late. Mike waited up for him but had decided to try a different approach. In the past, he waited by the door for David, becoming increasingly angry. David, anticipating his father's wrath, would grow more and more anxious as he neared home. When he opened the front door, he and his father would get into a loud and angry verbal exchange.

> Another important discipline factor involves giving choices. This approach increases a child's sense of control and lessens the need for a rebellious or confrontational response.

This time, however, Mike chose to handle the situation differently. When David came in, Mike simply glanced at his watch and said nothing, then went upstairs to bed. The next morning when emotions had cooled, Mike told David that he had a choice to make: He could either come in on time or stay home the following Saturday night. His behavior would determine which choice he made.

The problem was solved, and the Saturday night fights were a thing of the past. David felt as though he had some control, and Mike got increased compliance with the curfew.

Use Discipline to Teach

No parent particularly wants to discipline a child. And we have seen how disciplining when angry or at the wrong time or setting too tough a consequence can have destructive results. However, when used properly, discipline can teach our children lessons about their behavior. Keep in mind that the most important parenting goal is not necessarily instantaneous compliance with our wishes (although it would be nice), but to teach our children to be independent, responsible, happy adults.

Since our goal is to teach our children how to operate effectively in the world, discipline should be structured to teach our children lessons about their behavior. For example, Amanda, age sixteen, frequently borrowed her parents' car. Her parents are generally more than happy to lend it to her except that she often brings it home without replacing the gasoline that she has used. Her parents are greatly inconvenienced by her behavior since they often have to stop for gas in the mornings and consequently are late for work.

After discussing the problem, Amanda's parents decided that if Amanda returned the car without replacing the gas, they would restrict her from using the car for the next two days. They discussed their plan with Amanda. Of course,

Amanda did forget on occasion, and her parents, good to their word, took away the car keys for a couple of days. Before long, Amanda got much better at replacing the gas she used.

Amanda's parents accomplished two things. First, they modified Amanda's behavior so they would not have to be unnecessarily late to work. Second, they taught Amanda a valuable lesson: If you don't put gas in the car, it won't run!

Finally, when discipline is required, keep in mind that the goal is to change certain behaviors, not to prove who is right or wrong. Using this constructive approach promotes behavioral change, minimizes unnecessary conflict, and teaches our children important lessons about life.

> When discipline is required, keep in mind that the goal is to change certain behaviors, not to prove who is right or wrong.

Things to Remember
Using "Destructive Discipline"

- Don't attempt to discipline when angry.
- Use discipline at the proper time.
- Enforce appropriate consequences.
- Giving children choices increases their sense of competence and control.
- Use discipline to teach.
- The goal of discipline is not to prove that someone is right and someone is wrong. This approach promotes power struggles and enhances a child's sense of shame.
- The goal of discipline is to change problem behavior.

Self-Test 7

1. Don't attempt to discipline a child _____.
   A. When you are angry.
   B. When the child may not like it.
   C. During *Oprah*.

2. Using discipline when everyone's "psychological shields" are lowered involves:
   A. Self-confidence.
   B. Timing.
   C. Honesty.
   D. Trust.

3. Giving _____ increases a child's sense of control and lessens the need for a rebellious response.
   A. Advice
   B. Praise
   C. Choices
   D. Gifts

4. The goal of constructive discipline is to:
   A. Clearly establish who is right.
   B. Change problem behavior.
   C. Clearly determine who is wrong.
   D. Both A and C

5. If done correctly, discipline will:
   A. Scare your child into behaving.
   B. Prove that you, as a parent, know best.
   C. Teach a lesson.

Self-Test Answers

1. Don't attempt to discipline a child _____.

Answer A: Attempting to discipline when angry generally leads to hurt feelings, bad choices, and a general escalation of the situation.

2. Using discipline when everyone's "psychological shields" are lowered involves:

   Answer B: Timing is important to assure that the discussion will be heard and understood rather than simply defended against.

3. Giving _____ increases a child's sense of control and lessens the need for a rebellious response.

   Answer C: Giving children a choice empowers them and increases their self-confidence.

4. The goal of constructive discipline is to:

   Answer B: The goal of discipline of any type is to change problem behavior.

5. If done correctly, discipline will:

   Answer C: Children should learn from the consequences of their behaviors.

"Do As I Say, Not As I Do"

Earlier in this book, I related how my daughter, Lindsey, learned to make her bed at the age of four. She did a wonderful job, and as time went on, I remembered to praise her efforts periodically. Later, making her bed became one of the chores required to obtain her allowance. All was well in the bed-making department. Or so I thought.

When Lindsey was about seven, I noticed that her bed making had become much less consistent. When I remarked on the change, Lindsey looked at me and said, "But Daddy, you don't ever make your bed." I was surprised, but as I thought about it I realized that she was absolutely right. In recent months I had been getting up earlier for work and had been consistently neglecting to make the bed. The wonderful effects of those well-rehearsed parenting skills were out the window simply because I was not setting a good example.

Not surprisingly, as soon as I began to make my bed again, Lindsey quickly followed suit. I had forgotten to practice one of the most basic, yet powerful, parenting tools: modeling good behavior.

Parents hope that their children look up to them and give them love and respect. If parents are at all successful at obtaining their respect, they should not be surprised when children naturally follow their example.

If our behaviors have such a profound effect on our kids, then it behooves us to model desirable behaviors. If you are prone to swearing in traffic, don't be surprised to hear a few choice words from your child when a toy breaks. If you bend the truth on the telephone to get out of an unwanted engagement with a friend, don't be surprised when your child lies to you about a broken vase. If you smoke or drink and tell your children not to do so themselves, what do you think is the most likely outcome?

Alternatively, we can have a powerful positive impact on our children's lives by acting in ways that we would wish them to model. Our basic beliefs and values, those things that make up our character, are clearly communicated to our children through our daily actions. What we do has much more impact than what we say. Children seem to know instinctively that actions tell more about a person than do words. They are constantly looking for discrepancies between the two. If you think about it, many of your children's more probing questions stem from their confusion about what they have been taught and what they have seen.

> Our basic beliefs and values, those things that make up our character, are clearly communicated to our children through our daily actions. What we do has much more impact than what we say.

One father told me about an incident in which he walked outside and heard his daughter, Stephanie, speaking with her younger cousin. They were apparently catching "rolly-pollies," or pill bugs, and playing with them. Stephanie was admonishing her cousin to play carefully with the insects so that they would not get hurt and could be safely released. Later, this father jokingly asked Stephanie where she had learned to be so sensitive to the needs of a bug. She looked at him like he was crazy and said, "Daddy, I learned it from you. You always used to let butterflies go after we caught them." He was really taken aback. His daughter had learned a heightened sensitivity about empathy and the needs of others by watching him do something to which he probably hadn't given a moment's thought. She, in turn, reminded him to be aware that parents are constantly teaching their children, for better or for worse.

This lesson is critically important. By following the principles illustrated thus far in this book, parents are not just practicing techniques to get their children to behave better. They are also teaching their children valuable lessons about life and character. If a child is raised with a cooperative parenting approach, he or she will learn to be more cooperative with others. If a child sees a parent respecting the feelings and desires of others, that child will be more likely to do so as well. If a teenager's opinions have been listened to and valued, that teenager will be more likely to listen when a parent has something to say.

Just such a situation occurred with a fifteen-year-old client, Denise. Her parents divorced when she was young, and now she lived with her mother, who worked as a secretary. They came to my office because her mother complained that Denise was being smart-mouthed and unruly. She reported that Denise didn't do her chores, ran around with friend of whom she didn't approve, and regularly stayed out past her curfew.

After getting the background information from her mother, I spoke with Denise alone. She appeared to be a very resentful and defensive young woman. She angrily recalled that her mother had rarely taken time to listen to her as she was growing up. Her mother had dated regularly, and Denise had gotten the distinct impression that going out on dates was more important than spending time with her. Her attitude was "Why do I have to listen to her? She has always thought that her friends and her dates were more important than me."

It turned out that Denise's perceptions were basically justified. Her mother had always led an active social life and was frequently away from home. When she was home, she spent a great deal of time on the telephone planning her next outing or just gossiping with friends. Her behavior had sent a clear message to her daughter. She had unwittingly communicated that Denise's needs were not very important. Now that she was old enough to do so, Denise was responding with a message of her own. Using behaviors learned from her mother, she was saying, "My friends and desires are more important than you!"

The Media's Impact

In my practice, parents also ask me about the possible negative influence that the media, in various forms, may have on their children. They are understandably concerned about the sex and violence on television and in movies. They wonder whether the lyrics in popular songs will incite their children to violence or cause them to use drugs or alcohol.

These parental concerns have been the subject of volumes of research. The preponderance of this research suggests that the media does indeed have an effect on the behavior of children and teens. As they grow older and begin to search for their own identities and value systems, children, teens in particular, will begin to look to outside influences including peers and the media for information. Unfortunately, this search may lead them to incorporate some negative values and behaviors.

There is some good news, however. In the absence of other significant life problems, most teens will flirt with other values, beliefs, and behaviors but will eventually return to the values with which they grew up. If parents have actively taught their children solid values, through both word and deed, most will eventually adopt these same beliefs as young adults.

On a practical level, parents want to know what to do about these influences. Should I restrict my child's television? Should I let my children only listen to certain types of music?

I believe that children should definitely be shielded from information that is not age-appropriate. A five-year-old should not be exposed to the violence and sexual content of an R-rated movie, for example. However, children, and especially teens, should be allowed exposure to age-appropriate material, even if it is somewhat objectionable, as long as their parents are available to offer the proper guidance.

> In the absence of other significant life problems, most teens will flirt with other values, beliefs, and behaviors but will eventually return to the values with which they grew up.

As parents, we shouldn't be trying simply to shield our children from all negative influences, but instead help them develop values and skills that will let them better cope with life's challenges as they arise. Teaching our children strategies to evaluate and deal with competing situations and ideas is also necessary because parents will not always be around to screen them from potentially objectionable material. Parents who try to overly restrict their children's exposure without giving them evaluating tools will be at a loss when their children encounter restricted material at a friend's house. Isn't it preferable to have your child view the material and then want to discuss it with you when he or she gets home?

The key, as discussed in an earlier chapter, is to nurture a relationship with your children that allows you to communicate openly with them about issues of concern. This ability to communicate allows you to guide your children through this material and instill values and beliefs about it that will serve them well in later life.

A situation common to many of my clients will illustrate what I mean. Some very concerned parents came to my office complaining that they were having constant battles and power struggles with their fifteen-year-old son, Brent. They were concerned with the possible negative effects of Brent's friends, whom they did not like, and that the music he preferred would influence him to do drugs, have sex, or break the law.

Understandably, Brent resisted his parents' attempts to control his behavior. He complained that they did not trust him and that he wanted to choose his own friends and listen to the music that he liked. The situation became a crisis when his parents attempted to remove some CDs that they had discovered in his room because they contained sexually explicit lyrics.

Brent's parents had taken a parenting approach that led to conflict, resentment, and power struggles. By focusing on Brent's possession of the CDs, they had unintentionally created something over which Brent and his parents could struggle. The more important issues of communication, sexuality, and values had been overshadowed by a power struggle about perceived rights.

At my suggestion, Brent's parents reluctantly agreed to let Brent listen to any music he wished. They also agreed to sit down with Brent and have a discussion about sex, drugs, and values. The conversation was not to include mention of his music or friends, just general information about values and choices.

Within several weeks, Brent had stopped listening to the objectionable music because it had lost its shock value. He even admitted that he never really liked the music, but he felt that he had a right to listen to it and was willing to fight his parents to establish that right. Several more weeks passed. Then Brent's parents came into the office amazed about a recent discussion that Brent had initiated with them. He had come to them to ask their advice about what to do when an acquaintance of his had offered him drugs at school!

By changing their tactics, Brent's parents had modeled several important behaviors. They had shown Brent that they were willing to let him learn and that they trusted that he would make the correct decisions. They had also modeled the fact that they were concerned about his welfare and open to discuss any problems that he might experience.

Children may look up to sports figures, musicians, teachers, or even their peers. They are taught by television and the movies about different values and perspectives. But without a doubt, the most powerful influence on a child's growing sense of values and self are the actions of that child's parents.

Actions Do Speak Louder Than Words

Parents give daily messages to their children about morals and values. Despite what you say to your child, your actions have far more lasting impact. If you tell your child not to drink and have a few too many on Friday night, your child gets a powerful message. If you consistently break the speed limit or cheat on your taxes, your child is also getting a lesson in values and morals that far outweighs anything you might say.

The way we treat others is also powerfully communicated to our children. Vince is the father of a sixteen-year-old teenager, Ron. Vince works at a high-pressure job and tends

---

Things to Remember

"Do As I Say, Not As I Do"

- Model appropriate behavior for children by setting a good example.
- What parents do has more impact on children than what they say.
- Parents can model both positive and negative behaviors for their children.
- Children and teens may be influenced by peers and the media but will generally adopt the values and behaviors communicated by their parents.

to be harried and stressed at work. When he comes home, he is frequently on edge and irritable and consequently tends to snap at his wife when things don't go right around the home. When he came to my office, he was actually surprised that Ron tends to talk back to him!

When we treat others with kindness and generosity, we are showing our children the value we place on our relationships. We can teach them a similar, and more damaging, lesson when we are petty and selfish in our dealings with other people. If we tell white lies to get out of an unwanted engagement or have our children tell a caller that we are not at home when we don't wish to speak with someone, we are writing a blueprint that our children will use when they need to choose between being honest and dishonest.

As much as we may wish it not to be so, parents have to be constantly aware of the messages we send our children with our actions. The values that we model today will be the values and actions that our children will display tomorrow. So, if the clerk at the local convenience store gives you too much change, what are you going to do?

> As much as we may wish it not to be so, parents have to be constantly aware of the messages we send our children with our actions.

Self-Test 8

1. _____ refers to showing positive behavioral examples to children.
   A. Lecturing
   B. Giving advice

   C. Modeling
   D. All of the above

2. Which of the following has the most impact on a child's behavior?
   A. What a parent says
   B. What a parent does
   C. The media
   D. What Mr. Rogers says

3. Can the media influence a child's behavior?
   A. Yes
   B. No
   C. Only *Sesame Street* can

4. Which has the most influence on a child in the long run?
   A. Parental behaviors and values
   B. Values and behaviors learned from peers
   C. Values and behaviors learned from the media

Self-Test Answers

1. _____ refers to showing positive behavioral examples to children.

   Answer C: Modeling behavior gives children the message "Do as I do."

2. Which of the following has the most impact on a child's behavior?

   Answer B: Each of these answers has some impact on a child's behavior, but parental actions, by far, have the most long-term impact.

3. Can the media influence a child's behavior?

   Answer A: The media in the form of television and music have been shown to have influence on children's behavior.

4. Which has the most influence on a child in the long run?

   Answer A: As they reach adulthood, most people tend to return to the primary values that were taught and modeled by their parents.

Overlooking
Special Needs

Children experience a wide variety of emotions and exhibit some seemingly strange behaviors. Fortunately, most of these feelings and actions are relatively normal and can be adequately handled with consistent, positive parenting skills. However, since children don't usually come with an owner's manual, parents often find it difficult to know when a behavior is truly out of the ordinary and needs special attention or outside help.

All children are wonderfully unique. Each child has a different constellation of strengths, weaknesses, interests, skills, and vulnerabilities. Through a combination of life experiences and natural predisposition, children differ in their levels of activity, shyness, assertiveness, ability to tolerate frustration, and a myriad of other personality factors.

As children grow older, parents generally become increasingly aware of their children's unique personality traits. Some of these traits are quite positive and should be encouraged. Other tendencies can be potentially problematic and should be modified. The secret is to figure out which traits should be encouraged and which should be redirected.

A child who is very active physically might be encouraged to explore sports as a logical extension of his or her natural ability. If a child shows an interest in music, by all means encourage that interest. However, if a child seems reserved and prefers more intellectual pursuits, he or she should not be forced into situations, like sports or public speaking, that make him or her excessively uncomfortable.

Most children who are otherwise healthy do tend to exhibit some behaviors that might cause them trouble in the future. Parents, knowing their own child's unique personality makeup, should be alert for these behaviors and make appropriate attempts to modify them.

For example, Lindsey has sometimes exhibited a strong need to please other people. While a desirable trait in moderation, I wanted to assure that she did not need to rely too much on other people's opinion to feel good about herself. So when I noticed that she became excessively upset after bringing home an 89 in math because "It's not an A," I immediately assured her that it was her *effort* that impressed me, not whether she actually earned an A.

Sometimes children develop behaviors that indicate a more serious underlying problem. Often, parents have a difficult time distinguishing a minor problem or a passing phase from one that may require more intense or specialized intervention. Some general principles may help.

A parent may need to be concerned about a seemingly problematic behavior if it lasts for an

Often, parents have a difficult time distinguishing a minor problem or a passing phase from one that may require more intense or specialized intervention.

extended period of time or if it is of unusual severity. It may also indicate a deeper problem if the behavior significantly interferes with a child's daily functioning.

In my practice, I encounter many children who do, in fact, need special attention. Many of these children would have been better helped if treatment of the problem had been addressed earlier in the child's life. Some children already have significant problems with self-esteem and a greatly impaired sense of personal competence by the time they reach my office.

I certainly am *not* blaming parents for being unable to recognize the problem and not seeking treatment earlier. In the vast majority of cases, the parents were reacting as they thought best and had no way of knowing the child needed additional intervention. They simply did not have access to the information that would have alerted them to the problem and directed them to the appropriate assistance.

It is simply not possible to adequately cover all special problems that a child may encounter in a few pages. However, I will outline some of the most common problem areas so that parents may recognize the behaviors in their children and seek the appropriate treatment. What follows are some of the more common problems that I encounter in my practice treating children and adolescents.

Attention-Deficit Hyperactivity Disorder

Tommy began to scream and throw temper tantrums as a young child. Unlike most children, Tommy didn't grow out of his "terrible twos." When he entered school, he had difficulty staying in his seat and would blurt out answers in class. He always seemed to be in trouble with the teacher and frequently got into conflict with his peers.

Diane never really had behavioral problems at home or school. Her teachers seemed to like her, and her grades were fine. When she reached the third grade, her teachers began to complain that she would daydream in class and didn't seem to be paying attention. By the fourth grade, Diane's grades had fallen off considerably and she frequently didn't finish her assignments. It became harder for her parents to get her to do her homework.

Both Tommy and Diane suffer from attention-deficit hyperactivity disorder (ADHD). This condition affects from 5 to 10 percent of school-age children in the United States, which makes it one of the most common disorders of childhood and adolescence. It occurs three times more often in boys than in girls.

Children with ADHD have symptoms that fall into one of two major areas: inattention and hyperactivity/impulsivity. In these examples, Tommy's condition was characterized primarily by his being overly active and impulsive. Because his behavior was so disruptive, it was relatively easy to notice. Diane's behavior, in contrast, was characterized primarily by problems with attention and concentration. Her problems were manifested much more subtly and consequently were more difficult to spot. Some children exhibit symptoms of inattention, hyperactivity, and/or impulsivity in varying degrees.

In general, children with ADHD have difficulty filtering out auditory or visual stimulation, which makes it difficult for them to focus, especially in the classroom. If you think about it, a classroom is full of distractions—twenty-plus kids, instructions from the teachers, bells, announcements on the public address system, banging lockers, and noise in the hall.

Children with attention problems are often disorganized and do not complete their work at school. If they are given more than one chore to do at a time in the home, they frequently become sidetracked before they complete the initial assignment. They may be impulsive and accident-prone. Their schoolwork may be sloppy and inaccurate.

Many of these children tend to interact with their peers better in a one-on-one situation than they do in a group. They may have difficulty waiting their turn or may be "bossy." Group play situations may result in temper outbursts, fights, or hurt feelings.

Having ADHD can be extraordinarily difficult for a child. These children are usually brighter than average and thus become extremely frustrated when they are unable to succeed in class or at home. Imagine getting worse grades than others in your class when you actually understand the material. Then imagine that the teacher continually makes statements such as "You never apply yourself," or "You're lazy," or "If you would only pay attention and turn in your work." Then imagine going home and being punished for getting in trouble at school. Under these circumstances, it wouldn't take long until you gave up altogether!

Many parents ask, "Don't all children show these signs occasionally?" The answer is yes. However, in the case of ADHD these symptoms are the rule rather than the exception.

It is very important to have a child who exhibits the characteristics just

> Having ADHD can be extraordinarily difficult for a child. These children are usually brighter than average and thus become extremely frustrated when they are unable to succeed in class or at home.

described evaluated as soon as possible for the possibility of having ADHD. If allowed to continue untreated, children with ADHD can become frustrated and disinterested in school. They have a higher incidence of dropping out of school and developing problems with substance abuse and the law because they are unable to get the positive attention from parents, teachers, and peers that they need to develop a strong sense of self.

ADHD is generally thought to be a hereditary neurological problem. Many times I have been describing a child's symptoms to the parents, and Mom or Dad is frequently nodding and comments, "That sounds just like me."

If you suspect your child may have ADHD, you need to have him or her evaluated by several professionals. Unfortunately, no single test such as a blood test or urinalysis exists to determine whether a child has this disorder. Often a child is taken to a psychologist who can take a thorough history, make behavioral observations, and administer specific diagnostic tests. The child's behavior in *multiple settings* must be considered. Consequently, input must be obtained from parents, teachers, and appropriate professionals.

If a child is found to have ADHD, a referral is made to a pediatrician, pediatric psychiatrist, or pediatric neurologist to see whether medication may be helpful. The most commonly prescribed medications are central nervous system stimulants like Ritalin that can dramatically improve a child's ability to stay focused and concentrate. A psychologist can also help the parents learn to take behavioral steps to help the child succeed and to coordinate with and educate teachers, counselors, and school principals.

Children diagnosed with ADHD respond best to motivation, structure, and positive reinforcement. They need to be rewarded for staying on task and behaving appropriately. Many of the concepts discussed earlier in this book like catching children being good, consistency, modeling, and structure are especially important for these children.

Teachers who have ADHD students in class can help them by engaging in the following steps:

- Clearly display classroom rules.
- Post daily schedules and assignments.
- Forewarn students of schedule changes.
- Seat the child with positive peer role models.
- Plan demanding subjects for morning hours.
- Use breaks as incentives for staying on task.
- Mix high- and low-interest activities.
- Use a multimedia and multisensory approach.

Successful management of children with ADHD requires careful diagnosis and the intervention and cooperation of parents, teachers, and appropriate health care professionals.

Learning Disabilities

At fourteen, Doris always seems a little different than other children her age. She tends to be very shy and quiet, rarely interacting with other children. She is very reluctant to try new things and has always disliked going to school. She hates both reading and math because the numbers and symbols always seem to get "jumbled up."

Will also has difficulty in school. He especially dislikes having to speak in front of the class or write book reports. Unlike Doris, he doesn't have any difficulty understanding reading or math. Instead, he just can't seem to convey what he knows to others. When he attempts to write an essay or summarize a book in front of the class, he knows what he wants to say, but he just can't seem to make it come out right.

Dennis, now thirty-five, has always had difficulty understanding what people say—the words people spoke to him tended to all sound alike. His parents quickly became frustrated and often yelled at him for not paying attention or just being lazy. In school, he had difficulty understanding assignments. He began to fail most of his subjects and eventually dropped out of school at age sixteen.

Doris, Will, and Dennis each have a learning disability.

A learning disability is a disorder that affects a person's ability to interpret information correctly from the environment or to link information successfully from the different parts of the brain. Learning disabilities have nothing to do with a child's intelligence. A child can be very bright and still have a learning disability.

You might think of learning disabilities as you would a computer system. A computer system consists of the computer itself, the keyboard, and a printer. The computer can be likened to the brain. It may work beautifully, but someone with a learning disability may have difficulty processing information from the "keyboard," the environment. Conversely, they may have difficulty getting information from the computer to the "printer," the parts of the brain responsible for verbal or written expression.

> A learning disability is a disorder that affects a person's ability to interpret information correctly from the environment or to link information successfully from the different parts of the brain.

Learning disabilities are a lifelong condition. In many cases, they profoundly affect many aspects of a child's life such as schoolwork, daily routines, social interaction, or family life. Other children have very specific learning disabilities that have little day-to-day impact.

Children with learning disabilities have many of the same problems with behavior that children with ADHD exhibit. In fact, many children with ADHD have one or more learning disabilities. Having a learning disability can be extremely frustrating for a child who may have difficulty succeeding in school and thus getting positive attention from teachers and parents. A child's self-esteem can be significantly impacted.

If your child has consistent problems with one of the areas described here, it is important to have the school or a psychologist do a comprehensive evaluation to assess specific problem areas. The process will generally consist of a comprehensive intellectual evaluation (an IQ test) and several tests of achievement in specific subject areas. If a child's performance in a particular area does not conform to what would be expected of a child with a given IQ, the child may have a learning disability and require specific intervention. Learning disabilities generally do not respond to medication and cannot be "fixed." Instead, the key is to enlist the help of the school and focus on the ways the child learns best.

I used to work with a very bright and energetic woman named Diane. At the time that I knew her she was very successful in her career and in life in general. However, I learned that this had not always been the case.

Diane grew up thinking she was stupid. She constantly struggled in school. By the time she graduated from high school, she was convinced that she would progress no further academically. Luckily, she was tested when she applied for a local community college. Diane discovered that she was extremely bright but had a specific learning disability: She had extreme difficulty retaining what she read. It's no wonder she had such difficulty in school!

Through trial and error, Diane learned to compensate for her disability. She discovered that if she read her assignments into a tape recorder, she could retain the information. She was overjoyed to learn that she could experience academic success simply by finding another way to absorb information, a way that worked for her. She went on to obtain a master's degree and has never looked back.

Schools are generally required to accommodate children with specific disabilities or special needs. Most schools offer special education classes with teachers who are specially trained to help children with learning disabilities. Sometimes simple classroom modification is required such as giving a child more time to take a test or letting her do homework on the computer.

Although children with learning disabilities may need specialized academic help, they need love, attention, and positive feedback most of all. It is important to understand that learning disabilities are, in fact, life disabilities. They interfere not only with a child's academic development but also with many aspects of a child's life. Focusing on your child's special and unique talents and abilities to build a strong and positive sense of self is always essential to good parenting. It is especially important to children with learning disabilities.

Childhood Depression

Marla had always been such a sweet child. Her parents agreed that her behavior had always been exemplary. She always did well in school, had several friends, and was respectful to adults. Now, at age eight, Marla seems to be an altogether different child.

For the past several months, Marla has begun to complain about school. It is increasingly difficult to get her out of bed in the mornings. She has started to become irritable and edgy, frequently snapping at her parents and mumbling under her breath when she is asked to help around the house. She does not call her friends as often as before. When her friends do come to the house, they often get into squabbles and fights. Marla is depressed.

As adults, most of us have some idea of what it means to be depressed or down or to have "the blues." Often these reactions are quite understandable, as a reaction to some recent event. For example, it would be unusual to not feel some depressive symptoms after a loved one dies.

In adults, these depressive feelings can become more pronounced and lingering, prompting a diagnosis of major depression. An adult is considered depressed when he or she displays several of the following symptoms over several months:

- Loss of interest in normally pleasurable activities
- Increased isolation
- Low energy or fatigue
- Poor concentration and/or difficulty making decisions
- Poor self-esteem
- Poor appetite or a prolonged tendency to overeat
- Sleep difficulties
- Feelings of hopelessness
- Persistent thoughts about death or dying

Although we don't always recognize it, children can also experience depression. It is much more difficult to tell when a child is depressed, however, because children are far less adept at verbalizing how they are feeling. Consequently, they tend to show their depression in behavioral ways.

A child who is depressed may not be able to accurately tell a parent how she feels. Instead, she may show signs of increased withdrawal, changes in appetite or sleep, changes in social interaction, increased irritability, lethargy, or falling grades. The key to recognizing childhood depression is to look for a *significant change* in normal behavior that lasts for several weeks.

Keep in mind that all children, like adults, go through normal changes in mood. A bad week at school or being sad after a pet dies does not justify a diagnosis of depression. Again, it is important to look for significant changes in a child's behavior that last for a period of time. A child, like an adult, is more likely to experience clinical depression if depression runs in the family.

Parents who have noticed some of the changes described here and are concerned that their child may be depressed should definitely explore the possibility. A prudent initial step might be to call the school counselor and teachers to ask whether they have noticed changes in behavior or grades. It may be a simple explanation such as the child's best friend is now playing with someone else. On the other hand, the teacher may have noticed changes that are cause for concern.

A concerned parent should contact a qualified mental health professional who can help assess your child. If a diagnosis of childhood depression is made, psychotherapy can be effective in helping a child work through the problem. In some cases, medication may be helpful too.

When the depressive symptoms are due to a situational factor such as the loss of a pet, a grandparent's death, or a friend's move to another city, parents can do a great deal to help their children work through their feelings. If the child is younger than age ten, she may have trouble verbalizing exactly how she feels. Parents can encourage, but not push, their children to express their feelings by discussing their own feelings or how they felt in a similar situation. The parent should not tell the child how to feel but let her know that whatever she feels is normal and that the parent is willing to listen. It is also helpful, at times, to discuss with the child the positive memories about the object of the loss.

> Parents can encourage, but not push, their children to express their feelings by discussing their own feelings or how they felt in a similar situation.

Childhood Fears and Anxieties

Everyone experiences fear and anxiety. In fact, fear is a healthy and adaptive response that helps us avoid dangerous situations. Fear becomes problematic when it exists in response to things imagined or interferes with normal, everyday functioning.

In children, certain fears are common at certain stages of development. Here is a partial list of normal fears and their usual age of occurrence:

Age	Source of Fear
0–6 months	Loud noises
6–9 months	Adults other than primary caretakers; falling

2 years	Thunder; monsters; large objects (cars, trains, etc.)
3 years	Animals; the dark; being alone
4 years	Large animals; parents leaving (at night, to go to work, etc.); the dark
5 years	The dark; falling; dogs
6 years	Monsters, ghosts, witches; robbers; someone or something under the bed; medical and dental procedures

These and similar fears are common to many children and should not be of particular concern unless they persist much longer than expected and/or if they are of extreme intensity and interfere with normal functioning. Most children will grow out of them. Parents should simply reassure the child and continue with the normal routine. A child should not be allowed to avoid bedtime because of a fear of monsters, for example. This avoidance will only serve to reinforce the fear and make it much more difficult to calm the child (and get him to bed!).

Simple Phobia

A simple phobia is characterized by a persistent fear of a specific object or activity, most often dogs, snakes, and spiders. Other common phobias include a fear of heights, closed spaces, and flying. A fear is only considered a phobia if it causes extreme distress or interferes with normal functioning.

School Phobia

A common phobia seen by mental health professionals that is not listed as a formal diagnosis is school phobia. This phobia is manifested by a child refusing, or being extremely reluctant, to attend school. This child will often go to great lengths to stay at home, including complaining of illness or injury when nothing is medically wrong.

Treating Phobias

All phobias can generally be treated quite easily by a psychologist or other mental health professional. Treatment usually consists of exposing the child gradually to the feared situation or object through imagery and then in the real world. Teaching the child to make more positive and adaptive self-statements is also beneficial.

Self-statements are the things that we tell ourselves every day, usually without even being aware that we are doing so. Some examples might be "Wow, this pizza is hot" or "That's a nice car." This internal voice is particularly active when we are feeling afraid or insecure. Self-statements that increase our anxiety might be something like "There's no way I can speak in front of all those people" or "I just know something bad is going to happen today at school." Teaching children to use this internal voice to make more positive and affirming statements helps them control their fears and insecurities.

Overanxious Disorder

This is another type of unhealthy anxiety that exists when a child experiences persistent and unrealistic anxiety about a variety of things over an extended period of time. This type of anxiety can involve an excessive need for reassurance, perfectionism, fear of rejection, and excessive worry about past or future events. This disorder is most common among children whose parents have planted mental mines that tell them that they must achieve at a certain level to win acceptance and approval.

Obsessive-Compulsive Disorder

This condition is closely related to the generalized anxiety present in an overanxious disorder. Children with this disorder are generally more anxious about future events or things that have occurred in the past.

Some children who are generally anxious develop rituals and repetitive behavior patterns that they use to reduce their anxiety, such as washing, counting, or repeating verbal incantations. Again, these rituals may not be a problem unless they begin to interfere with daily functioning. When the rituals do disrupt daily life, parents need to seek the help of a mental health professional.

Consider the case of Terrance, whose mother brought him in to see me. At age ten, Terrance began to stay up increasingly late performing a stylized bedtime ritual. He would have to zip his book bag twenty times, turn off and on the light, and check each object in his room before going to sleep. By age eleven, Terrance was staying up so late performing rituals that his school performance suffered significantly.

After several weeks of therapy, it became clear that Terrance had an extreme fear of failure, of not measuring up. His parents were both very bright and had done well in school. After failing a test because he had been ill and had little chance to study, Terrance became extremely afraid of a repeat performance. After working with Terrance on more adaptive strategies and with his parents in terms of communicating more realistic expectations, Terrance is now a happy A/B student.

Like other childhood problems, many anxiety disorders can be prevented if parents strive to communicate openly with their children and give them a strong sense of unconditional love. Children need to know that their level of performance is distinct and separate from parental acceptance and love. The good news for those children that do develop anxiety disorders or unrealistic fears is that they are very responsive to appropriate treatment by a qualified mental health professional.

Like other childhood problems, many anxiety disorders can be prevented if parents strive to communicate openly with their children and give them a strong sense of unconditional love.

Conclusion

I sincerely hope that as a parent, you do not have to confront any of the problems listed in this chapter. However, a significant minority of children will experience one or more problems that require special assistance. For those parents who do have to confront these issues, it is important to educate yourself about your child's specific condition. The more you know about the condition, the better you will be able to serve as your child's champion and advocate.

Being a parental advocate for a child with ADHD, a learning disability, or an anxiety disorder is extremely important. Most educators and many professionals are not well versed in each of these conditions. It is up to the

Things to Remember

Overlooking Special Needs

- Many children will experience behaviors and moods that may seem odd but are actually transient and normal.
- A minority of children will experience symptoms of other conditions that will require the intervention of mental health, medical, and/or academic professionals.
- A parent may need to be concerned about an apparently problematic behavior if it lasts an extended period of time, if it is of unusual severity, or if it interferes with a child's daily functioning.
- Some conditions that may necessitate parents seeking outside help are as follows:
    Attention-deficit hyperactivity disorder
    Learning disabilities
    Childhood depression
    Overanxious disorder
    Obsessive-compulsive disorder
    Phobias
- If their children have unique needs, parents will need to serve as aggressive advocates for their children.

parents to serve as an advocate and educate the necessary people about their children's unique needs. The value of coordinating the efforts of medical professionals, mental health professionals, and the school cannot be overemphasized. As a parent, it is your responsibility to carry the banner for your child.

Self-Test 9

1. The majority of apparent problem behaviors that children exhibit are _____ stages of development.
   A. Normal
   B. Abnormal

2. Parents should be concerned about potentially problematic behavior if:
   A. It interferes with normal daily functioning.
   B. It occurs over an extended period of time.
   C. It is of unusual severity.
   D. All of the above

3. Children with _____ have difficulty filtering out auditory or visual stimulation, which makes it difficult for them to sustain attention and concentration.
   A. Attention-deficit hyperactivity disorder
   B. Learning disabilities
   C. Childhood depression
   D. Overanxious disorder
   E. Phobias
   F. Obsessive-compulsive disorder

4. Symptoms of this disorder include fatigue, isolation, sleep difficulties, poor self-esteem, and loss of interest in pleasurable activities.
   A. Attention-deficit hyperactivity disorder
   B. Learning disabilities
   C. Childhood depression
   D. Overanxious disorder
   E. Phobias
   F. Obsessive-compulsive disorder

5. Children with _____ may have consistent difficulty in major subject areas or with left-right differentiation, visual-spatial problems, or concept formation.

A. Attention-deficit hyperactivity disorder
B. Learning disabilities
C. Childhood depression
D. Overanxious disorder
E. Phobias
F. Obsessive-compulsive disorder

6. Children with this disorder have a persistent and unrealistic fear of a specific object or activity.
A. Attention-deficit hyperactivity disorder
B. Learning disabilities
C. Childhood depression
D. Overanxious disorder
E. Phobias
F. Obsessive-compulsive disorder

7. Children with this disorder tend to rely on rituals to reduce their anxiety level.
A. Attention-deficit hyperactivity disorder
B. Learning disabilities
C. Childhood depression
D. Overanxious disorder
E. Phobias
F. Obsessive-compulsive disorder

8. Children with this disorder are generally very anxious about most future and/or past events.
A. Attention-deficit hyperactivity disorder
B. Learning disabilities
C. Childhood depression
D. Overanxious disorder
E. Phobias
F. Obsessive-compulsive disorder

Self-Test Answers

1. The majority of apparent problem behaviors that children exhibit are _____ stages of development.

   Answer A: Children have many situational behavioral problems that do not require professional intervention.

2. Parents should be concerned about potentially problematic behavior if:

   Answer D: Parents should consider seeking additional information or assistance if one or more of these conditions are present.

3. Children with _____ have difficulty filtering out auditory or visual stimulation, which makes it difficult for them to sustain attention and concentration.

   Answer A: Attention-deficit hyperactivity disorder can have a hyperactive component or simply involve problems with attention and concentration without the hyperactivity. This condition is particularly problematic in a school setting.

4. Symptoms of this disorder include fatigue, isolation, sleep difficulties, poor self-esteem, and loss of interest in pleasurable activities.

   Answer C: It is important for parents to be aware of these symptoms because children have difficulty putting their feelings into words.

5. Children with _____ may have consistent difficulty in major subject areas or with left-right differentiation, visual-spatial problems, or concept formation.

   Answer B: Learning disabilities can have a profound impact on academic achievement and self-esteem.

6. Children with this disorder have a persistent and unrealistic fear of a specific object or activity.

Answer E: Phobias can include many stimulus objects including insects, school, a trip away from home, flying, or separation from parents.

7. Children with this disorder tend to rely on rituals to reduce their anxiety level.

   Answer F: Some rituals are normal in younger children and only become problematic when they begin to interfere with normal functioning.

8. Children with this disorder are generally very anxious about most future and/or past events.

   Answer D: A child with an overanxious disorder is fearful and stressed much of the time.

Forgetting to Have Fun

As adults, we often forget what it was like to be a child. We get caught up in the daily grind of trying to make a living, paying the mortgage, and raising our children. We forget that our children have valuable lessons to teach us as well. If we are sensitive and aware, our children can show us the wonder and excitement in our lives that we have all neglected to one degree or another. They can remind us how to live in the moment.

Children experience their lives with a wondrous sense of immediacy. They rarely think about what happened a month ago or what may happen next week. They spend each day exploring their worlds through sight, sound, touch, smell, and fantasy. Their world is alive with magic, wonder, and a powerful sense that anything is possible.

The people whom I have encountered in my life who are truly happy are those individuals who have actively fought to hold onto their childlike qualities. As the world tries to burden them with obligations, facts, rules, and a rigid sense of what is right, they strive to maintain an open and fluid enchantment with life.

In my profession, it can be alarmingly easy to become overwhelmed by the volume and magnitude of the problems that I assist people to confront each day. However, I am always mindful of the many times that Lindsey has brought me back into the moment by her playful and delighted approach to life. Whatever weight I might be shouldering quickly evaporates as I watch her chase butterflies or climb a tree. The gleam in her eye as she reads a new story or the way she squeals in delight on a carnival ride never fails to propel me into her world of sensation, motion, and enchantment.

Lindsey and I have a running joke about who is the real "Toys R Us" kid. She and the other children I have worked with have helped me reawaken the child inside—and I am immensely grateful!

I think that parents need to foster, along with independence and responsibility, that natural sense of playful curiosity and wonder that children naturally bring to our lives. And how better to teach them to value this wonderful ability than to join in the fun? Lindsey still talks about the fantasy trips that we took in our private airplane (her twin bed and a Frisbee for a steering wheel) or the castle in which we spent many a rainy night (blankets draped over the bed and the chair). When we engage in these fantasy games, we are really there, experiencing all the adventure and joy of being together on each odyssey. She taught me to be a child again,

> **P**arents need to foster, along with independence and responsibility, that natural sense of playful curiosity and wonder that children naturally bring to our lives.

and I showed her that being a responsible adult can be fun and exciting.

Teaching children to cherish and enjoy each day helps inoculate them against a host of potential problems in the future. Research has shown that adults who employ humor in their daily lives are healthier. Their immune systems are more robust, and, consequently, they get sick less often and tend to heal more quickly. Helping children learn to laugh at themselves teaches them to take life's inevitable setbacks less seriously. They will be less prone to be depressed, anxious, or compulsively driven. They will be more centered and happy.

For parents, the trick is to be very conscious of being in the moment with our children. It is far too easy to interact with our children but actually be thinking about what happened at work or when to find time to cut the lawn. Remember, children learn far more from what you do than from what you say.

Being in the moment means grabbing each minute and living it to the fullest. It means finding joy in whatever is right in front of you, in even the little things. Children learn this concept from their parents at a relatively young age. If they see you being distracted and distant, they learn that what is happening now is not very important or is something that should simply be endured. On the other hand, if they see you being actively involved and engaged with them or with what you are doing at a given time, they learn to focus on the now. It teaches them to be happier, more content, and more enthusiastic.

Even mundane tasks can be opportunities for fun and excitement. Making games out of chores or singing while you sweep the patio can teach children how to live in the here and now. It helps them be more content with themselves rather than thinking that something (or someone) better is just around the corner. Show your children how to cherish being in the immediate moment, and you will discover that you have a happier and healthier child. Besides, this attitude makes parenting much more fun!

There are several things that I hope you have gleaned from reading this book. First, parenting is not a passive process. It should be an extremely high priority. Good parenting involves being an active part in our children's lives. And whether we are conscious of it or not, most of what we do as parents significantly impacts our children. Again, being a parent is not something you *are*—it is something you *do!*

Once you make the commitment to be an active parent, the experience can be one of the most rewarding that you will ever have. I see many clients who complain about their jobs, their marriages, and their children. However, I have never encountered a client who has actively raised a child state that he or she regretted the experience. Many of us learn as much from our children as we are able to impart to them.

The role of a parent begins, and to a great extent remains, that of a teacher. Showing children unconditional love, guarding against planting mental mines, and openly cooperating and communicating with them is a daily exercise in positive instruction. Even consistently enforcing consequences and managing incentives teaches our children valuable lessons about the way our world operates.

As children get older and move into their teen years, our direct control over them decreases. Consequently, our

> **O**nce you make the commitment to be an active parent, the experience can be one of the most rewarding that you will ever have.

parental role shifts somewhat from that of a teacher to that of a guidance counselor. A wise parent recognizes this natural progression and strives to be available to guide and nurture teens as they struggle with becoming independent and responsible adults. During this process, open communication, reflective listening, and problem-solving approaches are the most valuable parenting tools.

The bottom line:

- Choose to make parenting a priority.
- Be active in your child's life.
- Teach positive lessons with word and deed.
- Learn from your children.
- Have fun!

Self-Test 10

1. Children experience an intense sense of:
   - A. Being in the moment.
   - B. Déjà vu.
   - C. Lethargy.

2. Far too often, parents get caught up in the daily pressures of life and forget that parenting can be:
   - A. Tiring.
   - B. Expensive.
   - C. Fun.

3. The proper role of a parent should be that of a:
   - A. Boss.
   - B. Teacher.
   - C. Talk-show host.

Self-Test Answers

1. Children experience an intense sense of:

   Answer A: Children have a wonderful way of experiencing events very intensely as they happen. Parents can learn a great deal from this ability.

2. Far too often, parents get caught up in the daily pressures of life and forget that parenting can be:

   Answer C: Parents who make raising their children a priority and who have the ability to be in the moment with their children find parenting to be much more rewarding than those who take a passive parenting stance.

3. The proper role of a parent should be that of a:

   Answer B: The foremost goal of parenting should be to teach children how to be independent, responsible, and happy adults.

Index